You Can Be Free

an easy-to-read handbook for abused women

based on the national bestseller *Getting Free*

Ginny NiCarthy and
Sue Davidson

SEAL PRESS

To honor the memory of Ruth L. Crow
for her enlightened work on behalf of girls and women.

You Can Be Free
An Easy-to-Read Handbook for Abused Women

Published by Seal Press
An Imprint of Avalon Publishing Group, Incorporated
1400 65th Street, Suite 250
Emeryville, CA 94608

9 8 7 6 5 4 3 2 1

Library of Congress Cataloging in Publication Data

NiCarthy, Ginny.
You can be free : an easy-to-read handbook for abused women / by Ginny NiCarthy and Sue Davidson.
p. cm.
"Based on the book Getting free: you can end abuse and take back your life by Ginny NiCarthy."
ISBN-13: 978-1-58005-159-0
ISBN-10: 1-58005-159-6
1. Abused women—United States—Handbooks, manuals, etc. 2. Abused wives—United States—Handbooks, manuals, etc. I. Davidson, Sue, 1925- II. NiCarthy, Ginny. Getting free. III. Title.

HV6626.2.N48 2006
616.85'822—dc22
2005027361

Cover and interior design by Domini Dragoone
Printed in the United States of America by Worzalla
Distributed by Publishers Group West

Contents

Safety Plan for You and Your Family

Chapter 1 explains the safest way to use the safety plan so it will help to read it first. Your safety plan must fit your personal situation. Try to combine this general safety plan with what you know about your own life. As you look at each item, ask, "Will this keep *me* safe?" "Can it put me in more danger?" "How can I use it so it is safe for *me*?" Then write down the plan in whatever version will work best for you. Weigh the benefits and dangers of taking each step of the plan against the benefits and dangers of *not* taking it.

Plan for an Emergency: Where Can You Go?

Make this plan *before* an emergency happens:

- Think of a safe place to go if you are attacked or threatened. It could be a neighbor's house, a police station, or somewhere open all night. Try to make it a place where you can call a friend. The friend should be part of your early planning.
- Practice how to get there. If you can get away in a car, keep the key with you all the time. If you have to walk or take a bus, check out the route at night. Is it safe?
- If you live close to a neighbor, talk to her about a signal you might give if you are in danger. It might be banging on a wall in a particular way. It could be shouting a word, or a telephone call with a coded message.
- Pack a bag with important papers, medicine, extra clothes, money, and things for your children. See the list in Chapter 7 and the additions to it in the chapters on immigrants, Deaf women, and those with disabilities.

- Memorize telephone numbers of the National Domestic Violence Hotline, 800/799-SAFE (800/799-7233) and 800/787-3224 TTY, and of your local shelter or hotline.

In an Emergency at Home

- Try to get to a room that has a way out.
- If that is impossible, try to get to a room that has a phone and a door that locks.
- Stay out of the bathroom or kitchen, which contain possible weapons such as razor blades and knives.
- Use the plan (above) that you made to escape the house.

Safety at Work

- Tell trusted coworkers about danger you are in.
- Tell them about phone harassment on the job.
- If it seems safe, tell your boss. Ask for help with your safety plan.
- Ask your boss to make your work phones secure.
- If you take a bus, ask a coworker to walk to the station with you.
- If parking lots are not well lighted, ask to have the lighting improved
- Ask a security guard or other employee to walk you to your car. Show that person a picture of the person who abused you.
- If you drive, take a different route each day.

Safety for Children

- Teach your children how and when to dial 911.
- See "Helping Your Children Be Safe at Home" in Chapter 14.

Chapter 1

△

Introduction

If you are being hurt by an intimate partner, you may be wondering how you got into this fix. You might even wonder whether you are an "abused woman." If that is the case, what can you do about it? How can you get your partner to stop mistreating you? Perhaps you are thinking that your life is nothing like what you hoped for—and neither are you. Maybe you wish you could get back to being the person you used to be.

You Can Be Free can help you build a more satisfying, safer life. Right now, you may be afraid of being struck or beaten. You probably feel humiliated or depressed a lot of the time. Sometimes you may feel very angry. These feelings can drain you of most of your energy. All this makes it hard to think clearly, much less to plan a safe way out. Reading this book can give you some breathing space, help you sort through your emotions and needs, and give you some tools for making changes and reaching your goals.

Recognizing Abuse

Abuse means mistreating another person. Abuse may be physical, emotional, or sexual. The word "abuse" can be used to mean each of these things. Or it can be used to mean all three of them.

Physical abuse is battering. "Wife beating" is another name for it, though many who are battered are not wives. Battering is not just one hit. It's a pattern of physical assaults, threats, or restraints. It is violence used to control another person. Men who batter scare women into doing what they want them to do. A person who batters almost always uses emotional abuse, too.

Emotional abuse is mistreating and controlling another person through feelings. It includes insulting, giving orders, and saying things to confuse the partner. The emotional abuser makes the partner feel afraid, helpless, or worthless. A person can be abused emotionally in many, many ways. Chapter 2 will tell you a lot more about emotional abuse.

Sexual abuse is mistreatment by means of sexual acts, demands, or insults. It can be partly physical and partly emotional. Or it can be only one or the other.

Abuse is a pattern of control. You might call a black eye, a bruise on your arm, or a small cut a "minor" wound. But any kind of abuse might keep you from leaving temporarily or permanently. It serves as a warning. Each time you see your bruise you are reminded to do as you're told. "Stay put. Don't you dare go to the store alone or visit your mother. Don't even think of separating for good." Your fears can keep you under the abuser's thumb as well as a broken hip can. If you are afraid, you will probably do what he wants. He may not even need to hit you again. He's got you where he wants you. So any injury can have serious consequences.

An abusive person uses whatever is handy to frighten you. You may be afraid of many things. Maybe poverty is one. Or being hit. Or being abandoned. Or fear that if you leave you will be stalked. You might be most afraid for the safety of your kids. The abuser will know. He will threaten to take your kids away. He will say you can never support yourself. Or that your health is so bad, no one would want you. If you are an immigrant, he may take your green card and say he can have you deported.

It is hard to recognize certain kinds of threats. They creep up gradually. That can happen when you are humiliated or intimidated. In time that might mean you lose a sense of your value. An abuser might keep you from developing your abilities. Then you feel worthless. You gradually stop taking any actions. You are trying to be safe. But you don't realize that it is also risky not to take action. To be safe means more than just avoiding physical injury. To be safe, you have to be free to make your own choices. You need to stay away from anyone who tries to control you.

The Importance of a Safety Plan

We offer suggestions for how to increase your safety whether you stay with the abuser or leave. But let's start with what you can do if you decide to leave. It is important to make a safety plan first. If he—or she—has struck you or threatened to, the violence likely will get worse when you say you are going to leave. He might do everything possible to stop you.

An abuser may interfere with your mobility. Anything that makes it hard to get around on your own puts you at risk. He may break your leg. If you live in a rural area, there may be no public transportation. A car may be your only hope of getting away. The abuser knows that. He may disable your car. When he leaves home, he might take the phone with him. In an emergency you may have to take extreme action. Planning for it can make all the difference.

You need to plan to be in a place where he cannot find you. If you have children, it is urgent that you work out plans to protect them. It may be helpful to view all of *You Can Be Free* as a safety plan. The chapters help you build emotional strength. They give you ideas on how to strengthen ties to people who support your independence. We offer suggestions about how to value yourself and find others who appreciate you. We suggest steps that help guard against injuries and threats to your life. Any of those actions may be your first steps to safety. In an emergency, you might make a different choice. You might run to a neighbor's house. You are the one who knows what you *can* do. You can figure out what is most important to do first. Even though you will do most of the hard work, many people may help you. One of their main contributions can be in working with you on a safety plan. For example, hot-line workers will help you find women to talk to, who can speak your language, who are part of your community. They will listen, they will offer information, and they can help you make a safety plan.

Many safety plans for abused women are available in books such as *Getting Free*. Others are online. Many of the tactics may be new to you and worth trying. They can protect you from being attacked or killed. They offer good advice about how to leave safely. See the basic safety plan that precedes this chapter. Consider how the basic plan fits your individual situation. But first, we hope you will finish this chapter. It will help you gain perspective on the value of a safety plan.

Uses and Limitations of Safety Plans

Guidelines can help you figure out how to cope with terrifying circumstances. But they are not rule books. You may even face risks in *following* those general guidelines. They can save your life, but unless you carefully evaluate how they will work for you, they can increase your danger. You have to factor in your situation. Your plan will be shaped by the abuser's traits and your responses. It will be affected by your emotional and physical condition. Availability of services will have a big impact. For instance, how quickly can you get help from police, family, or friends? Your community's reactions can make a big difference, too. You can develop a safety plan that is right for you now. Then as your life changes, you can adapt it.

General safety plans can be useful. But they have limitations. They usually advise you to call 911. They tell you not to get trapped in a room without a second exit. Stay out of the kitchen. But those ideas do not allow for your personal situation, because there are too many variations. What if your partner is pointing a gun at you? Reaching for a phone could save your life. Or it could increase your danger.

Think seriously about the suggested plans. But consider alternatives. Maybe in the past you "talked down" the abuser. That might be a safer choice than trying to reach for the phone.

The general safety plans advise you to arrange a signal to a neighbor to call police. But what if your neighbors are too far away to get the signal? You know what has happened before. You know how your partner reacts to your attempts to be safe. That information is invaluable in figuring out a workable plan. You can combine it with the ideas in the general safety plan to fit your needs. Some chapters address special situations:

Sarah created a safety plan that suited her best. She was blind and Deaf and not able to predict her husband's violent episodes. When her husband's anger escalated, her guide dog pawed Sarah. She thought the dog needed more training. But an advocate helped her realize the dog was agitated because he knew she was in danger. She made a new safety plan. When the dog got upset, she would calmly say the dog needed to go out. Then she would stay away from the house until her husband's violent impulse receded.

This story illustrates the kind of plan that can emerge when you brainstorm with an advocate. Such a highly individual safety plan would never show up on a standard list, but it worked for Sarah. (All names are fictional. Some details have been changed for the women's safety. A few stories are composites.)

Taking the Steps to Safety

A safety plan is useful only if you can use it. That may seem obvious. But the police or the aid car might take an hour to respond to your call. That won't keep you safe and could even increase your danger. You might have to make another choice. Think of saving your life as the goal at the top of a ladder. Your life is the most important thing. Even so, you may have to climb other steps first. What will it take to reach your goals? Consider the risks of taking each step.

Think also about the costs of *not* taking the step. You may be worn out, humiliated, depressed, or injured. Maybe you don't feel ready to approach even the first step. But with help, you can do it. Maybe it will be something you never thought you could do.

Other people may try to talk you out of what you are doing. They may not understand what your goals are or why you are taking steps they regard as trivial. Some of them may want to help you. They may be right about the dangers of staying. But try to help them understand the dangers of leaving too. It can be more dangerous to leave unless you have a solid safety plan. More women are killed during or after separation than when still with the abuser. Either choice could risk your life or those of your children. If you leave and are not able to stay away, you might return to an even more dangerous situation. But a carefully made safety plan can keep you out of danger.

Making an Emotional Safety Plan

You may face serious physical injury almost every day. But there are many other kinds of danger. Living with an abuser can cause you to lose your independence. Your self-confidence drifts away. You may not notice it. Nearly all abusive people want to gain control over their victims. The best way to accomplish that is to isolate you. The abuser may first tell you he loves you too much to share you with your friends. Next he says your family is a bad influence. Pretty soon you hear only his opinions. When he says you are stupid, ugly, or no good, you begin to believe him. Once that happens, it is easy to shame and humiliate you. You become depressed. You begin to believe you deserve to be abused. By then you might have lost contact with people who could help. If that has happened, he has succeeded. He may not even have to use physical threats to control you. Being under his power and control begins to feel normal.

Think hard about whether that has happened to you. Chapter 2 will help you discover whether it has. It also gives you ideas about how to recognize the emotional abuse and to react to it. Watch for signs that a person wants to make you feel helpless. "Helping" can develop into controlling. Keep doing things for yourself, even when you feel worn out.

Your first step in your safety plan might be to tell the abuser you know what he is doing and insist he stop. But consider the risks of speaking up. Might he punish you more? Have you tried it before? What happened? If he reacts with violence, do you have a plan to protect yourself? To get your kids to a safe place? To make a sound safety plan, you need to weigh your risks. You will need reliable information about your options. A domestic violence advocate can help you find it. Listen to knowledgeable people. Then make your own decisions.

You may not be quite ready to speak up. It could take time to clearly identify the problem. If you think *you* are the one at fault, you need first to learn to talk to yourself in a nonabusive, constructive way. Remind yourself of the traits you most value in yourself. Don't believe anyone who says the things you enjoy are stupid or useless. (See Chapters 2 and 9.) As you can see, a safety plan can be complicated.

Working with an Advocate

Talking over your situation with a friend or relative can be useful. So can consulting a doctor, lawyer, or counselor. But talking to people who don't understand can be risky, too. Before you ask for help, try to find out how the person feels about abuse of women. If she blames you or doesn't believe you, she can harm you more than helping. The safest person to confide in is likely to be a domestic violence advocate. She has the kind of experience you most need. She has learned from her training and from listening to other women. She understands that you are the one who knows most about the abuser. She can ask questions that encourage you to appreciate your best qualities. Talking with her can enable you to find the strength to solve your problems. With her broad experience and your specific information you can work together. You can figure out the best way for you to reach your goals.

> *"But I'm different. I'm an immigrant. I don't speak English."*

> *"I'm Deaf."*

> *"I have physical disabilities."*

> *"This is just the way things are in my rural/ethnic/ religious community."*

If you are in any of those situations, you are "different" from the mainstream. But you are also very much like many abused women. Your advocate will know about challenges for an abused woman in your community. She can tell you how likely the police are to respond quickly to a 911 call. That can be crucial in a rural area. She will know what their general attitudes are toward women who are battered. She may also know how they treat immigrants. She might know their attitudes toward people with disabilities. Or women who have several children and rely on public assistance. If she doesn't have the information, she will know how to find it. If she doesn't offer, ask her to refer you to someone who does know.

Advocates' Questions

An advocate will rarely give you advice. But she can help you evaluate the degree of risk you face. She might ask what you want to happen. Many women want two important things. They hope to stay with their partner and they want to be safe. Discussions with an advocate might enable you to decide which is most important. It could help you see how you can make it happen. She might ask about what you have already tried to keep yourself safe. What has worked? What hasn't? Can you change the tactic so it works better? If you try that, might it put you in more danger? As you hear your own answers, you gain new perspectives. That will help you make a safety plan.

Maybe you'll decide that you have to choose between your relationship and your safety. With ideas from the advocate you can list advantages and disadvantages of each possible choice. (See Activities 3 and 4 in Chapter 7.) Pooling your information, you and she can weigh the risks of each option. You can identify the first steps to take to reach your goals.

Shelters

An advocate can tell you where the nearest shelter for battered women is. Even if that option seems too extreme, it might feel good to know it's possible. If you do decide to go to a shelter, she can arrange it. She will know whether the staff has what you need. Maybe it's access to a language interpreter. It could be kosher food, legal information, a private place to pray. If she doesn't know, she can find out. When a shelter does not have what you need or want, staff will usually find a way to provide it.

In some areas the shelter is a big house where several women live for short periods. An advocate is available for information about legal and other issues. Other areas have Safe Homes, where one woman and perhaps her children stay in a private home. They may be welcome for a week, a month, or longer. The hosts may be very well informed about abuse. At the very least they are in touch with experts on abuse. Their most welcome trait might be an ability to listen.

Safety Plan: Step by Step

First, decide what goal sits at the top of your stepladder. Safety? Saving the relationship? Protecting the kids? Having enough money to get along? Being free? Once you are clear about the goal, don't keep looking up at it. If the climb looks too steep, you might give up before you start. Focus instead on the first step. Put your foot on the lowest rung. Then the next rung. And the next. If you feel stuck, enlist a friend to help. Don't worry about choosing just the right first step. If it isn't perfect, you can change it. Do what you *can* do. If your physical safety is endangered, do whatever is likely to keep you safe for a short while. Give yourself time to make a longer-term plan. If you are not in physical danger, focus on ways to strengthen your confidence. Increase your energy. Give yourself some pleasure. Fix yourself a treat. Pick some flowers. Read a story to your child. Take a walk. In other words, get moving. Do something different. It will give you energy and make the second step easier.

Take the second step; it could be calling a neighbor. The third might be asking her over for coffee. These may not seem like safety steps, but they are. They lead you toward taking control of your life. Take the steps one at a time. If you need smaller ones in between, take them. At each point, weigh the risks. Do what seems right for *you*. After you have taken a step or two or three, notice how far you have come. You may not be very high yet. But not long ago, you were afraid to get off the couch. Now you are on the steps.

Keep going. That will be the next challenge. For the first few steps you might want to stay close to an advocate or friend. Choose someone who can be your cheerleader. She has to know where you are headed and to understand the risks involved. She has to appreciate how hard some steps are for you. She will want you to achieve what you want for yourself. As you travel up the ladder, the abusive person will probably try to stop you. The less he knows about what you are doing, the safer you may be. But even if you are knocked down, you can always get up again. Begin again and again, if necessary. A good safety plan can keep you and your children out of danger.

Before you continue reading, look at the safety plan. Consider each item. Ask yourself which is safe for you. Which is not? Then make a tentative plan. You can change it as you read the rest of the book.

Reading this Book

We begin Chapter 2 with a method of identifying emotional abuse. Then we consider abuse in society. Next come several chapters on what you can do about it. Finally, we guide you through activities designed to change your life. Most chapters apply to all abused women. Several chapters apply to women in special situations: women with children, teens, lesbians, rural women, immigrants, women with disabilities, and Deaf women. You might turn to the chapter that best fits your situation. Then you can refer back to the chapters written for a general audience. Or you can read the book straight through.

You will find quotations from women who have faced challenging situations. But you might be surprised at how strong women are. They have faced barriers to safety similar to your own and surmounted them. You can be strong enough to do that too.

We could not write about all the challenging situations women endure and overcome. You might face barriers to safety that we have not mentioned. But any time you say, "I'm different," remember that others have experienced similar situations. We hope you will see how the circumstances we describe apply to your own life. The book will not tell you what to do. We hope it will help you discover what you want to do. Then it suggests ways you can make that happen. We know the path you will take will not be an easy one. But we also know that many women have paved the way for you. Through this book, they speak to you. Like them, you too can be free of abuse.

Chapter 2

△

Emotional Safety Plan

Many of the activities in this book could be called emotional safety plans. The table of contents will show you where to find all the activities. If you have been emotionally abused, your confidence may be melting away. Activity 1, beginning on the next page, and others in chapters that follow can help you regain it. You may have gradually lost your emotional strength. Think of the activities as emotional free weights. You lift a few more each day. You get emotionally stronger. That won't necessarily keep the abuser from trying to harm you. He might even punish you. But you will have more strength to confront him.

The first part of your emotional safety plan is to see and admit the danger. The first seven categories of questions in Activity 1—A through G—help you recognize what the abuser does to you. Check each question with the answer that fits: "Often," "Sometimes," or "Never." Then do the same with the last two categories. They show you the effects of the emotional abuse.

Activity 1 *Emotional Abuse Checklist*

A. Isolates You

1. Does your partner get angry when
   you talk on the phone?   ____   ____   ____

2. If you speak a non-English language,
   does he try to prevent you from
   using it to talk to friends or family?   ____   ____   ____

3. Does he keep you from seeing
   friends?   ____   ____   ____

4. If you live in a rural area, does he
   disable your car when you want to
   go to town?   ____   ____   ____

5. Does he insist that you stay home
   with him whenever he is there?
   Claim that it's because he loves you?   ____   ____   ____

6. Does he "save you the trouble"
   of running errands by doing them
   for you, so you never get outside
   the house? Does he do you a favor
   by talking to others on the phone
   for you, claiming that it is too hard
   for you to speak English, or to use a
   TTY, or to maneuver a wheelchair to
   reach the phone?   ____   ____   ____

B. Insults and Humiliates You

7. Does he call you names such as "dumb Indian," "bitch," or "welfare queen"?   ____   ____   ____

8. Does he tell you that you are too incompetent or helpless to get along without him?   ____   ____   ____

9. Does he say no one else would want you?   ____   ____   ____

10. Does he tell you in public that you look foolish? When you are using American Sign Language (ASL), for instance?   ____   ____   ____

11. Does he force you to do things that make you feel ashamed?   ____   ____   ____

C. Threatens You

12. Does he threaten to hurt your children or to get custody of them?   ____   ____   ____

13. Does he say he will kill himself if you leave him?   ____   ____   ____

14. If you are an immigrant, does he say he will have you deported?   ____   ____   ____

15. Does he say he won't let you leave the house unless you have sex with him first?   ____   ____   ____

continued

16. Does he raise his fist if you
    challenge him?   ____   ____   ____

D. Insists on Obedience and Petty Demands

17. Does he insist that meals be served
    precisely when he wants them?   ____   ____   ____

18. Does he insist that the house look
    just so all the time?   ____   ____   ____

19. Do you have to report how you
    spend every dollar?   ____   ____   ____

20. Does he time your trips to the
    grocery store? Keep track of your
    car mileage?   ____   ____   ____

21. Does he insist that he knows best when
    and how much medicine you need?   ____   ____   ____

E. Wears You Down; Wears You Out;
Fosters Feelings of Helplessness

22. Does he keep you up late, asking
    about men in your past?   ____   ____   ____

23. Does he interfere with technical
    equipment, such as a breathing
    apparatus, or withhold medicine so
    that you don't function well?   ____   ____   ____

24. Does he insist you constantly work
    at unnecessary tasks at work or

home, or both, so you never
can rest?   _____   _____   _____

25. *Does he insist you do hard tasks?*
    Then, if you are tired, does he say
    you are too weak to do them?   _____   _____   _____

This next category may not seem to be abuse. In the short run, "kind" treatment or promises to reform may seem a big relief. But through time they give you false hope. They may keep you in the relationship.

F. Does You Favors; Gives You Presents; Makes Promises

26. *After he has been mean, does he act*
    sweet and loving?   _____   _____   _____

27. *After he has hit you, does he give*
    you a present or take you out?   _____   _____   _____

28. *When you are finally about to leave*
    him, does he promise to change but
    fail to make a plan or act on it?   _____   _____   _____

G. Neglects You

29. *When you are sick, does he insist*
    you keep working?   _____   _____   _____

30. *Does he go out frequently and*
    refuse to say when he will be back?   _____   _____   _____

continued

31. If you have a disability or illness, does
    he "forget" to pick up your medicine?   _____   _____   _____

32. Does he take your only car and
    then "forget" to take you to
    appointments?   _____   _____   _____

How You React:
A. You Consider the Abuser Before Yourself

33. Do you worry about what he will
    think of what you wear, the makeup
    you use, or your hairdo?   _____   _____   _____

34. Are your decisions about whom
    you will visit or where you will go
    based on what you believe he will
    "approve"?   _____   _____   _____

35. Do you speak very carefully and
    "walk on eggshells" to be sure you
    won't upset him?   _____   _____   _____

B. You Feel Worn Out, Incompetent, Crazy, Helpless

36. Do you try so hard to make sense of
    his "crazy-making" contradictions
    that you are often confused?   _____   _____   _____

37. Do you feel sick, yet you're not sure
    what's wrong?   _____   _____   _____

38. Are you unable to do things you
    used to do easily?   ____   ____   ____

39. Do you doubt your own judgment?   ____   ____   ____

40. Do you sometimes think you
    are "crazy"?   ____   ____   ____

41. Are you afraid you can't manage
    your life without the abuser's help?   ____   ____   ____

Answers to the first seven categories of questions tell you what the abuser does. Your partner or caretaker may have used many emotional abuse tactics. Perhaps you answered "Sometimes" or "Often" to many of the last two sets of questions. Then you marked "Often" next to "doubt your own judgment." That tells you the abuse is beginning to work against you. The abuser is gaining control over you. *You can reverse that trend.*

Suppose you have begun to believe you are help-less. Then the second step of your emotional safety plan might be to tell your partner he is wrong. But consider, first, whether that can put you in more danger. Weigh the risks of confronting him against the risks of saying nothing. Which is more dangerous? "Saying nothing" might sound like a passive position. It doesn't have to be. It might just be trying out another tactic. You might change your second step to safety. Instead of confronting him, you might spend time with friends who know you can take care of yourself. Encourage them to remind you of that. They have to be the kind of people who know the difference between when you need help and when you are perfectly capable of acting on your own. Reaching out to people can ultimately save your sanity. It can save your life. And like every other action when your partner is abusive, it involves risk. He might react by using harsher tactics to isolate you.

Here is a different beginning step you can try. It is even risk-free. Change the way you talk to yourself. You can contradict what the abusive person says about you. What you say to yourself about who you are is extremely important. Turn to Chapter 9 and do Activity 5, the self-criticism list. If you would rather keep reading, do that activity later.

Your actions, as well as your talk, can make a big difference in how you feel about yourself. If your partner says you are stupid, you need to do things that remind you that is not true. Find ways to exercise your mind. If you can attend a class at a community college, that could help. First, you have to get out of the house. That might be hard to do. If you live in a rural area, classes may not be available. Don't give up. Look for something in your home, or something you can bring into it, to exercise your mind.

What if you have no books or magazines? Do you have, or can you get, a deck of cards? How about a Scrabble board? Crossword puzzles are in most newspapers. Experts say they are one of the best ways to keep mentally agile. Don't worry if you can't think of many answers at first. The more you do, the better you will get. The point is not to fill in all the squares but to exercise your mind by trying a challenging activity. Then you reinforce your actions by congratulating yourself for trying. One advantage of a crossword is that you can fold it into a small piece of paper. The abusive person does not need to know about it. Access to the Internet offers endless possibilities for stretching your mind.

These are just a few examples of what we call "emotional weight lifting." If you are called "ugly," "wetback," "useless," or "crazy," think of ways to contradict those messages. Substitute a statement that is true. Turn to Activity 5 again. You can do things to become physically strong, more rational, a good cook—whatever attracts you. You can find an advocate who will help you develop a program to do that.

You might think that the category of neglect doesn't lend itself to these steps. But it does. You can think of ways to take better care of yourself. If you don't eat well or sleep soundly, you weaken yourself. If you don't take your medicine, you put yourself at risk. An advocate can help you find ways to take better care of yourself.

The same principles apply to threats, intimidation, "crazy making," isolation, and the other forms of emotional abuse. As you read the rest of the book, you may come back to this chapter and to the ones that suggest activities to make you emotionally strong.

> Lisa is a Tlingit Indian, abused by two husbands (both white). About her second husband she said: "He would try to make love after he beat me. . . . After he beat me, he bought me things all the time. . . . I couldn't relate to anyone, couldn't explain how I could be locked into one little corner of my mind and not remember anything. It was like going crazy. . . . He moved out and we started making new lives, but he was at every one of the softball games I played in, just watching, making me nervous. Then he started . . . bringing me flowers."

Lisa did not fall for the flowers. She has a good job working for the state of Alaska. She is married to a man who treats her well. She got away from her abusive partner.

Chapter 3

△

Why Does Abuse Go On?

You may have concluded that you are being abused by your partner. If so, this book can help you. It can help you decide whether to stay or leave. It can help you solve new problems that you will face if you leave. It can help you build a safer, better life.

But you are only one woman among many. Millions of women are abused every day. How can this go on? Why does it happen? Can anything be done to stop it?

This chapter will help you see that changes are possible.

Background of the Problem

Until recently, many people thought men had a right to batter women. Wife beating was even protected by law. In some countries, the laws began to change. In the United States, wife beating became illegal early in the twentieth century.

But battering still went on. Most people thought it was a private matter. They didn't think society ought to meddle in it. Battering wasn't discussed in public. Nobody wrote about it. It was kept hidden.

Some people still want to keep battering hidden. They pretend it doesn't happen. Or that it's not serious. Or that the woman brought it on herself. Friends and relatives may refuse to see the problem. Doctors, lawyers, police, and judges also may ignore it. Is it any wonder a woman who is battered feels alone?

> *Jennifer remembers what it was like, feeling there was nobody she could talk to. People acted as if there were something wrong with* her, *not the batterer! She says: "I needed somebody to say, 'It's not your fault. You're not making him be this way and you can't make him* not *be this way.' Nobody was saying that. One friend's response was, 'Well, that's not really battering. It's not that serious. You didn't break any bones.'"*

Changing Attitudes

During the 1970s, women began to speak up about battering. They gave support to women who chose to leave violent men. They helped women who wanted to prosecute the batterers.

They insisted the public listen. More people began to admit that battering happened. More people began to see that battering wasn't just a private problem. They began to see that it was society's problem, too.

Now it has become possible to:

- Make laws to protect women who are abused
- Educate doctors, nurses, and counselors about abuse
- Educate police, lawyers, prosecutors, and judges about abuse

Still, people continue to ask, "Why do battered women stay?" Their tone might express anger or frustration. You might feel criticized. Maybe you have talked only about the terrible things your partner does to you. You may not have talked about his kindness. His ability to support you well. Maybe they really want to understand. Perhaps you have never tried to explain.

You could say something such as, "I'll try to tell you. But it is not simple. It will take a while." Then sit down for a long talk. Explain why you stay. Besides the valuable traits of your partner, there are plenty of other reasons. Maybe you're balancing the good times against the dangerous ones. Maybe you're afraid there is no one out there who is better. Maybe you believe separating will put you in even greater danger. Maybe your partner has threatened to kill you if you "abandon" him. Your friend probably doesn't know how dangerous it can be to leave without a safety plan. That might take time to complete.

You might have other fears, such as leaving your community. Your husband may have threatened to fight for custody of your kids. You're afraid of the struggle to support them on minimum wage. You might see yourself all alone, without support. You haven't explained why you are not prepared to leave. You haven't asked friends and family for help if you do separate. This is a good time to start asking.

In recent years many people have changed their attitudes about abuse. They have begun to understand why it is difficult to stop abuse or leave the abuser. Now some ask, "Why does he batter?"

Anger does not explain abuse. Most of the time, people who are angry don't hit anybody. "Anger management" rarely changes the abuser's actions. Many people think abusers are "sick." A very small number are mentally ill. Most are not. Besides, most mentally ill people are not violent or controlling. Maybe it's because he was abused as a child? Childhood experiences may *contribute* to abuse. But many abused children do not abuse as adults. Few abused girls grow up to become abusive adults. Stress is often said to be the cause of battering. Maybe he lost his job or he's worried about the one he has. But again, most people experience stress and they do not abuse.

Abuse is a matter of choice. People who batter are rarely "out of control." Instead, they want to be *in* control. They believe they are entitled to control women and children.

What Can Be Done?

The abuser might change if he really wants to. It is hard work. He will have to attend a batterers' intervention program for many months. He will have to stop being violent. And he will also have to stop being emotionally abusive. He can get help from an intervention group, but it is up to him to do the work.

More and more women are saying "No!" to battering and emotional abuse. They are changing laws. They are changing people's ideas. They have created new services. There are now many shelters, legal advocacy programs, and support groups. There are services for immigrant, Deaf, and rural battered women and for those with disabilities. You can read about some of them in this book.

△

Chapter 4

Is It Ever Right to Break Up the Family?

Maybe you've decided what you *want* to do. You want to leave the man who abuses you. But you're not sure it's what you *should* do. You may have thoughts such as these:

"A woman's place is with her man."

"A woman doesn't leave just because of a few fights."

"You can't run away from your problems."

"A family should stay together and work things out."

Whose Ideas?

Where do those thoughts come from? Are they your ideas or someone else's? Are they what your mother has said? Your husband? Your minister? Your counselor?

Once you know where the ideas come from, you can decide whether you agree. Do you really believe these things? Or do you just say them without thinking about what they mean? Do you think a wife should stick by her husband, no matter how he treats her?

You may decide that it's wrong to put up with an abusive man. But you're still not sure you should leave. You worry with thoughts such as these:

"He'll fall apart."

"He'll kill himself."

"I can't deprive him of the kids."

Will He Really Fall Apart?

People do "crack up." They do kill themselves. What are the chances that your worst fears may come true? No one can say. But some questions may help sort things out.

Has he "cracked up" before? Has he tried suicide or had a breakdown in the past? If he had mental problems before you met, you're not the cause of them now. He may crack up again if you leave. But he may be able to handle stress better now than before. Not everything he does depends on you.

Has he talked about suicide? It is not true that people who talk about suicide don't do it. You should take a threat of suicide seriously. It could mean great danger. If your partner is willing to kill himself, he may think he has nothing else to lose. Abusers who kill themselves sometimes murder their wives and children first. Try to force yourself to imagine it. Then you can make a safety plan to prevent it. You cannot stop him from killing himself. But you can take care of yourself and your children.

Even if you worry that he will kill himself, that does not mean you have to stay with him. Your first obligation is to protect yourself and your children. Physical violence is not the only danger to the children. Most men who abuse women through threats and emotional abuse treat their children in the same way. They humiliate and frighten them. Consider whether you want your children to grow up being treated that way.

What About the Children?

Suppose you have decided the best thing is for you and your kids to leave. Your partner may be very angry or hurt or scared. He may blame you for what he predicts will happen. "You're going to turn them against me." "They'll forget all about me."

Those complaints might make you feel too guilty to leave. But there's no reason to accept the picture he's drawn. A father and his children can be close without living in the same house. Their relationship will depend a lot upon how he acts toward them. He could stay involved and learn to treat them well. It depends on how he deals with the separation.

You may want to cut all ties with him. You may want to disappear so that he can never find you. But taking your children away without a court's permission can be very risky. You could be charged with kidnapping them. Then he might get custody. You wouldn't be able to protect them. And you might not be able to see them at all.

Abusive fathers sometimes threaten to kidnap children. Usually, it's an empty threat. But if your husband makes that kind of threat, you need legal advice.

Child Abuse

Are your children battered? Many adults think it is all right to hit children to punish them. They may not know child abuse when they see it. Sometimes child abuse is punishment that has gotten out of control. It's punishment that puts cuts, welts, burns, or bruises on a child. It can result in lifelong damage or even death. Often it has nothing to do with discipline. Abusers often think that they are entitled to control everyone in the family. That it's okay to humiliate others, including children. A child needs to be kept away from an abuser if at all possible. Children don't have the power to protect themselves. The abuser might humiliate or insult them frequently. They can suffer lifelong damage from emotional abuse too (See Chapter 14).

Sexual Abuse of Children

Sexual abuse of children happens in families of all classes and races. Batterers are not the only people who abuse children sexually. But it is not rare for them to do it. The victim may be a child of the abuser's parter only, or a child of the abuser too.

Don't depend on the child to tell you what has happened. The abuser has probably made threats about what he'll do if she tells. (Or if he tells—boys are abused, too.) If you suspect your child has been sexually abused, don't wait. Find a quiet place to be alone. Explain that some adults touch children in ways they should not. Be clear that when that happens, it is not the child's fault. Don't use words such as "bad" or "dirty." Ask a few questions and wait patiently for answers. Maybe there won't be any this time. Encourage the child to tell you if something does happen.

Some adults claim that a child can provoke incest by "sexy" behavior. That is one way to shift blame to the child. But it's the adult who has power over a child. It's the adult who is responsible for the abuse.

If your children are abused, you can take steps to protect them. The best way to do that may be to leave and get custody. But you have to be sure to make a safety plan. You can guard against your partner's getting custody by letting others know that he abuses the children. Take them to a doctor when the abuser hurts them. Do that whether or not they need treatment. Ask the doctor to record the injuries. You'll be able to use the record later if there is a custody dispute.

Chapter 5

△

What Do You Owe Yourself?

The person who abuses you acts as if you have no rights. So you're probably afraid to act as if you do. By now, you may not even think that you have any rights. But you do. This chapter will help you to realize what they are.

Are You Somebody Besides Wife, Mother, or Girlfriend?

Many women can't tell where the family leaves off and they begin. They feel they're just a part of the children or their husbands. They forget that they have a separate identity. Try to answer these questions:

1. What do I want?
2. What do I want to do now?
3. What do I like to do?
4. Whom do I like to spend time with?
5. What do I like to wear?
6. Where do I like to go?
7. Where would I like to live?
8. What do I want to be doing in five years?

9. What do I want to be doing in ten years? In twenty years?

How many of your answers were something like this?

"I want to live here because moving would mean changing the kids' schools."

"He likes me to wear . . ."

"I don't much care—I'm easy to please."

"My husband wouldn't hear of it."

"It costs too much."

If your answers are like that, you're not saying what you want. You're saying what other people want. Or you're implying what you think can't happen.

Try answering again. This time, don't think about how other family members would respond or would be affected. This doesn't mean you don't care about your relatives. It simply means that you deserve some things you want. It means that you count for something. You are a person, too.

After she left, Maddie began to see herself as someone important. "I could almost say I was born again. When I was with him, all I thought about was him and the kids. But when we were separated, I was in tip-top shape. I felt up!"

▲ △ ▲

Mind Reading

Women are taught to think of the needs of others. It's supposed to be part of their role—especially as wives and mothers. Young children can't say how they feel or what they need. Their caretakers—mostly women—have to figure out their needs for them. But adult men are able to say what they need or want. Why don't they do it? Why does a woman have to guess what a man is feeling?

It is partly because men are taught not to express emotion. That's why a man may depend on his woman to guess what he's feeling. Is he depressed? Frightened? Lonely? Does he want comfort?

An abused woman tries hard to read the abuser's mind. Her health and safety may depend on it. If she's not tuned in to what her partner wants, he may explode. However, some violent men explode even if their needs *are* met. You need to notice how far mind reading goes in making you safe. You also need to ask yourself if it's worth the strain. Do you owe yourself a chance at something better?

What If It's Really My Fault?

"I started it last time by nagging him."

"I'm a sloppy housekeeper."

"I'm cold in bed."

"Sometimes I hit him back."

"He puts up with a lot from me."

You're aware that you have faults, too. This makes you feel that you're responsible for the abuse. It may keep you from thinking of ending the relationship. Instead you may think: "If only I can change, he'll change, too."

But what changes will really keep him from hitting you? Make a list of things you did that he says "caused" him to hit you. Maybe the house wasn't perfectly clean. Or dinner was late. Or you spent time with women friends. Did you get hit every time you did those things? *Only* then? Were you hit sometimes for no reason at all?

Which of your "faults" do you want to correct? Do any of them give him the right to "discipline" you with a beating? Let's take as an example your spending time with women friends.

Do you deserve to have friends? Friends can give you what you don't get from your partner. Friends will talk to you and listen to you. They show they care about you and like you. Every person deserves these things. You may try to get along without the comfort you get from friends. But then you get lonely and depressed. So you take a chance and secretly meet your friend. If your partner finds out and beats you, does that mean you were wrong? Is it really a fault to want friends?

Does one adult have the right to punish another? No.

This right would mean that the man has the authority to control you. And to use violence to do it. *He does not have either of those rights.* Whether you have faults is beside the point. You are not his property or his child. In fact, the law now limits the rights of parents to punish children.

What Are Your Rights?

It's likely that you've given up your rights little by little. Perhaps you didn't even notice it was happening. Freedom of speech—a basic right—is usually the first to go. An abused woman stops talking about things that might upset her man. Here are some of the things you may have stopped talking about:

1. Past relationships—he gets jealous.
2. Dreams for the future—he thinks you're complaining about how things are now.
3. Questions about his work, what he's done, how he feels—he accuses you of prying or nagging.
4. Statements of your opinions—he doesn't want to hear what you think. "You're stupid."
5. Statements about feeling down, sad, lonely, or discouraged—he doesn't want to hear your complaints.

▲ △ ▲

It may be hard for you to realize what your rights are. Here is a list of rights that everyone is entitled to.

List of Rights

You have the right:

1. To state opinions, including unpopular ones
2. To express feelings, even if you feel down
3. To privacy
4. To choose religion and lifestyle
5. To be free of fear
6. To have some time for yourself
7. To spend some money as you please
8. To paid employment at fair wages
9. To choose your friends
10. To emotional support from family and friends
11. To be listened to by family and friends
12. To decide whether to have sex or not

Draw a line under each of the rights you think everyone deserves. Next, circle the rights you have now. Is there a difference between your rights and those of others? Does that mean that you aren't a person? Or does it mean that wives don't have rights? That women don't have rights? That mothers don't, until their children are grown?

For many women, it's hardest to believe they have rights to time and money. Let's look at these two.

Money

Perhaps there's not enough money to pay even basic bills. Still, some money is always spent on things that aren't essential. Does the grocery bag contain candy, pop, beer, or cigarettes? If so, someone has already made some decisions about what is "needed."

It's hard to decide how family money should be spent. But *both* adults should decide. Compromises can be worked out. Each person should have something to spend, no questions asked. The amount may be small. But it's hers or his to spend.

If you're sneaking money, you're acting as if you don't have rights. You're acting like someone who isn't allowed to make her own decisions.

Time

Each of you should have some time to spend as you please. It should be at least one half day and one evening a week.

You may not know what to do with your time at first. Take it anyway. Go to a movie that your partner doesn't want to see. Walk in the park, take a class. Doing what *you* choose will help you begin to build your own identity.

Getting Respect for Your Work at Home or for Pay

Some people still believe that the man should be the sole provider. They think of a woman's earnings as "a little extra." For most families, that's not true anymore. As living costs rise, most families need and use the woman's income.

Ideas about work have changed. More people have begun to accept the following ideas:

- Work is of equal value, whether done by a man or a woman.
- Women need adequate pay, just as men do.
- Both partners in a realtionship should share housework and child care.
- Work in the home is as important as work outside it.

Suppose your partner wants you to stay at home. Yet, he looks down on the work you do there. After a while, you might begin to agree.

If that's what's happening, you need to change something. You may need to relearn respect for your work at home. List all the reasons you think it's important. If you still don't believe it, you may need to look for a paid job.

Maybe you already work outside the home. But neither you nor your partner think it's important. In that case, you may need to get training for a better job. In other words, start respecting what you do or doing what you respect.

Claiming Your Rights

Look at the list of rights earlier in this chapter. Decide which rights you want to begin claiming. Is it safe to discuss them with your partner? You could start with agreements about time and money. Will he keep to his part of the bargain?

If the answers are no, you owe it to yourself to consider leaving.

You have rights, like anyone else. But you have to believe in them yourself. That's the first step in getting them.

Chapter 6

△

"But I Still Love Him"

Three kinds of love occur between partners in a couple:

- Romantic love
- Addictive love
- Nurturing love

At times, the three overlap. But they can be looked at separately, too.

Which kind of love do you and your partner share? This exercise will help you to find out. Put a check mark in front of each of the following that seems true.

Activity 2 *How Do You Love Each Other?*

_____ *1. I could never love anyone else the way I love him.*

_____ *2. Without him, I have nothing to live for.*

_____ *3. I know exactly what it is about him I love.*

_____ *4. I suppose I should be interested in other people and activities, but I just want to be with him.*

_____ 5. We help each other to explore new ideas.

_____ 6. Whenever I'm a few minutes late, he thinks I'm with another man.

_____ 7. I wear my "rose-colored glasses" and see only the best in him.

_____ 8. The thought of his being with anyone else makes me miserable.

_____ 9. I hope he never leaves me. But if it comes to that, I'll be okay.

_____ 10. He could never love another woman the way he loves me.

_____ 11. Often, I feel better when I'm away from him. But then I call him anyway.

_____ 12 I never let him see me without makeup or wearing curlers. I want him always to see me at my best.

_____ 13. He brings out the best in me.

_____ 14. I don't know why I love him, I just do.

_____ 15. He has many of the qualities I value. They are qualities I'm trying to develop in myself.

_____ 16. It's wonderful to spend time alone with him, and also together with others. I also enjoy being by myself and with women friends.

continued

_____ 17. *He's so special. I don't know why he's interested in an ordinary person like me.*

_____ 18. *Without me, he has nothing to live for.*

_____ 19. *He wants me to feel good whether I'm with him or not.*

_____ 20. *This time he means it—he's really going to change.*

_____ 21. *He wants to know where I am every minute. That's how I know he loves me.*

_____ 22. *I like to hear about the good times he has with other people.*

Romantic Love

Romantic love is supposed to be magic. It's supposed to go like this: Two people meet. They know at once that they were made for each other. They weren't meant for anybody else in the world. There's nothing they can do about it. They are helpless in the face of their love.

These ideas are very popular. We hear songs about them. We read stories and see movies about them.

Look at your responses to 1, 7, 10, 12, 14, and 17. The more you checked, the more romantic your ideas about love are. To keep them, you have to hide a lot from yourself. And from him.

You are deeply in love with the idea of your man. You don't want that idea to be shaken by his real behavior. Never mind the facts. He's wonderful. You're perfect for each other. He'll stop his cruelty soon. The magic of your love will go on and on.

Addictive Love

Romantic love can be experienced as a kind of "high." For some women, this is not dangerous. It's not dangerous for a woman who likes herself. It's not dangerous for one who values other friends and interests. If her man stops loving her, she'll mourn for a while, but her entire world won't fall to pieces.

But some women place a low value on themselves and their interests. Love overwhelms everything else in their lives. For such a woman, romantic love can cross over into addiction. Her world shrinks to nothing but her need for the man. She'll be certain she can't live without his love. She'll put up with anything from him, just to keep it.

Her life may become an addictive cycle. There is the "high" when her need for him is fulfilled. Then comes the "downer" when the "supply" is removed. She is completely dependent on getting her supply. She can't get it from anybody but him.

Sometimes the man, too, feels that he can't live

without the woman. They are addicted *to each other*. Men who batter are even more dangerous when they are addicted to the woman. They may go to any lengths to keep a woman from leaving.

Did you check 6, 18, and 21? These indicate that the man is addicted to you. Did you check 2, 4, 8, 11, and 20? Checks for these reflect your addiction to him.

Nurturing Love

Nurturing love is the opposite of addictive love. It promotes growth and strength rather than dependence. It is based on real appreciation of the loved one's good traits. But neither partner has to pretend that the other has no flaws.

Nurturing love helps each partner to improve. It expands the world of each. It does not cut off other relationships and interests.

Look at your responses to 3, 5, 9, 13, 15, 16, 19, and 22. The more of these you checked, the more nurturing your love is. The man in such a relationship may sometimes get angry at his partner (so may the woman), but he would not abuse his partner.

Can You Leave Someone You Love?

Loving an abusive man makes it hard to leave, but it's not impossible. The most loving thing may be to separate, even if it's temporary. Nobody wants her loved one to continue a round of violence. If the relationship is also an addictive one, your course is clear. To have a healthy life, you'll need to end the harmful one. But first be sure to have a safety plan.

If you want to leave, you'll need to give up certain romantic ideas. These are ideas such as: "He's the only one who can give me what I need." "I'll never find another man to love." "My life's not worth living if I don't have love all the time."

There was a time when Dee thought she couldn't live without Pete. Now she says: "I can remember years and years of saying to myself, 'I love this man; how can I help him?' I would never go back to him because I'm so happy now."

Chapter 7

△

To Leave or Stay: How to Decide

Some battered women read every word they can find on abuse. But the reading doesn't give them what they want. They hope to find a solution that doesn't require leaving the man. Or a solution that doesn't mean risk. Or one that won't bring pain.

No solutions are like that. If you change your life, it will bring you rewards. It will be challenging. It may even be exciting. But it may also be hard, lonely, and frightening, at first.

Are you serious about making changes in your life? If so, it's time to face the facts, and then act. The facts may not be as awful as you think.

What's the Worst That Can Happen If You Leave?

You may imagine terrible things happening: "I'll be so depressed, I'll take an overdose of pills." "I won't be able to support the children. Then I'll lose custody of them."

Maybe your fears are less dramatic: "How will I discipline the children by myself?" "I'll be stuck at my office job forever. I'll never be able to get ahead."

Perhaps your worst fears are more vague: "Being alone." Try to make the frightening thought specific. Is it sex you'll miss when you're alone? Someone to go places with? Someone to lean on and be needed by?

If you are an immigrant, you may be afraid of being deported. If you have a disability, you might fear that you can't get along on your own. If you live in a rural area or are Deaf, your concerns will be related to your circumstances. Considering them carefully can keep you safe. Chapters 18 through 21 can help you deal with those fears. You might want to read whichever chapter fits your life before you complete Activity 3 on the next page. The ideas there will help you fill out the worst fears list.

Write down your worst fear of what might happen. Then list reasons it's likely to happen, and reasons it's unlikely. For example, your worst fear might be "losing the house." A reason it's likely might be "can't meet the payments." A reason it's unlikely might be "can rent out rooms if kids double up."

Activity 3 *Worst Fears List*

Worst Fear:
_____

Reason it's likely:	Reason it's unlikely:
_____	_____
_____	_____
_____	_____

Make lists of what's likely and unlikely for each fear you have. You'll be sure of some of your answers. With others, you might need expert advice on what is likely or unlikely. It might be a question of property or custody rights. Or about getting welfare assistance or job training.

Expert advice isn't always expensive. In some cities there are low-cost services. Call these places to ask about free or low-cost services:

- A shelter or women's center
- Legal Services
- County Bar Association (lawyers' group)
- A crisis hotline

Be sure to mention that you've been battered. Sometimes there are special services for abused women.

Gather as much information as you can. Then return to your worst fears list. Make any changes your new information suggests.

What's the Worst That Can Happen If You Stay?

Think about the worst that might happen if you stay. Think of what might happen short-term and long-term. How will staying affect your children? Consider emotional as well as physical harm.

After she left, Hope saw how much her children had suffered. It made her feel sad to remember. "I'd say to my boy, 'Don't cry when Dad is home.' He was about five. I didn't know about being mentally battered. He mentally battered my boy."

Think back to the last time you were abused. List the things you were afraid of, starting with the worst. Were you afraid you might be killed? Crippled for life? What if you killed your man, as some abused women have? How would you feel later?

Try to imagine your future if any of these things happened. Do you get enough from the relationship to take such risks?

Looking at Both Sides

"Should I stay?" "Should I leave?" List the good things and the bad things about staying and about leaving.

Activity 4   *Leaving and Staying— The Good and the Bad of Each*

	Leaving		Staying	
	Good	*Bad*	*Good*	*Bad*
1.	_____	_____	_____	_____
2.	_____	_____	_____	_____
3.	_____	_____	_____	_____
4.	_____	_____	_____	_____
5.	_____	_____	_____	_____
6.	_____	_____	_____	_____
7.	_____	_____	_____	_____
8.	_____	_____	_____	_____
9.	_____	_____	_____	_____
10.	_____	_____	_____	_____

Some items might turn up on both lists. For instance, you might put "loneliness" on the "Bad" list under "Leaving." But you know you'll be lonely if you stay, too. But "seeing my friends" is unlikely to appear on both "Good" lists. And seeing your friends can do a lot to make you less lonely.

When you have finished the list, you may still be undecided. If so, score each *good* item you've written on a scale from 1 to 10. A 10 indicates that an item is very important to you. A 1 indicates that an item is of low importance to you. Do the same for the *bad* items. Then add the scores for the good items and the bad items. That should help you decide what you want to do.

The next step will be finding out *how* to do it.

What Can You Do If You Stay?

This section offers very general advice. See ideas on planning for safety at the beginning of the book and in later chapters that address specific situations, such as those of rural or Deaf women.

Perhaps you've decided you can't leave just yet. You don't have skills for the job market. You have no supportive people in your life. Your children are not yet in school. You think you have to take a chance on staying a while longer.

If you're serious about leaving later, make some changes now. Make a friend. Join a support group. Get job skills through on-the-job training, classes, or volunteer work. Otherwise, you'll be in the same position later as you are now.

Some men bully only those who are afraid of them. You may be able to do some "forbidden" things by just *doing* them. However, it's a risk. Plan an emergency escape to a safe place before you take that risk.

Many men are sorry right after they've battered. This is sometimes called "the honeymoon period." They're willing to give in to some things you want. This is a good time to get out of the house and meet people. It's a good time to start the changes you plan.

It may be hard to face new people with a black eye. Make yourself do it anyway. Once your bruises fade, it's easy for your man to forget what he did. You won't be able to count on his being sorry. You'll be afraid of being hit again if you try something new.

How to Plan for an Emergency Escape

Whether you plan to leave or stay, you'll be safer if you have an escape plan.

Learn to know the signs of coming violence. Do they begin weeks before the actual abuse, or only hours? Or minutes? *Write down the signs.* Write down changes in the way he acts or in his tone of voice. This will help to get you into action before the violence starts.

Where can you go for safety? The best choice is to the home of someone who cares for you—someone who will support you, no matter what you do. This might be a good friend or a relative. Otherwise, choose a hotel or motel *ahead of time*. Practice getting there from your house when you're not under stress. Also collect these things:

- Money for cab fare
- Change of clothes for yourself and/or children (hide clothes away from home, at a neighbor's house, or at your job)
- Money for one or more nights at a motel
- Extra house key and car key
- List of emergency phone numbers

Plan for a quick getaway, day or night. Find excuses to go outdoors that won't make him suspicious. Make a habit of taking out the garbage at midnight or walking the dog twice a day.

When you need to escape, pretend you're going to do one of those tasks. Then just keep going. Get into the car and drive off quickly. Or keep walking until you get to a phone.

If you have children, make plans for taking them. Tell the abuser you hear the baby crying. If you can, pick her or him up and leave from a back door or window. Prepare older children to go to a neighbor's house if you can't get away. They can call the police. Officers may help you leave with younger children.

If you must leave without the children, go back for them. Return to the house with a police officer as soon as you can. Or pick them up at school. Your right to custody may be endangered if they are not with you.

Preparing to Leave Permanently

After you have an emergency plan, you can think about leaving for good. If you plan to stay away, here are some practical things to think about.

Protect Your Money and Property

Laws about property rights for married people differ from state to state. They are also different for people who just live together. You'll need a lawyer's advice on what a court might award you and on what you can legally take with you. Then you need to plan how to get the things out.

Remove as many personal belongings as you can several weeks before you leave. Include photographs and sentimental objects, if you want them. Those are the things he might destroy.

Try to take important items to a friend. This may be too risky if the man notices everything you do. If he does, make a list of important things you want to take. (Don't forget items important to your children.) Move them little by little to two or three places in the house. Then you'll be able to pack them quickly when you do leave.

Remove your things when your partner isn't at home. Try to have a friend with you, in case he returns. Find out whether the police can be there. Other community agencies may also help.

Unless a lawyer says you can't, take half the money in checking accounts. Do the same with savings accounts. Don't leave your share of money in joint accounts to take out later. Your partner may withdraw all money from the accounts. He may take your name off credit cards. He may change all the locks. You could find yourself with no money or property twenty-four hours after you leave.

It's possible you don't know exactly what you and he jointly own. Look for papers that show stocks, property, loans, insurance policies you both own. Write down all the information. If you can do it safely, make copies of the papers. If necessary, give all papers and lists to a friend you trust.

It isn't mean or unfair to take what is yours. Don't deprive yourself or your children of what you need because of guilt feelings.

Plan Where to Go

Try to find a place to live before you leave. It might be one of these places:

- A battered women's shelter
- A friend or relative's home
- A Safe Home for abused women
- An apartment of your own

Battered women's shelters and Safe Homes are now in many communities. Chapter 13 tells how to find out about them.

Try to decide where you want to live permanently. You might want to move to a different city. Sometimes a local shelter can help you find temporary shelter in a new city. Check housing ads so you'll know what to expect in your price range. You may need public housing or welfare assistance. Find out what papers you'll need to show you qualify. Get them together to take with you.

The better you prepare now, the easier it will be for you later.

Chapter 8

△

Getting Help from Professionals

Many women in danger turn first to police. Usually that happens when they are scared and desperate. In a dangerous situation that might be the best thing you can do. But there are arguments against it too. We mentioned some of them in Chapter 1. In this chapter we suggest ways to think about the pros and cons. You may not want to think about them now. But it's important to be prepared. Then in an emergency you will know what to do. If there never is an emergency, nothing will be lost.

Do You Want to Involve the Justice System?

Lynn, an African American woman, answered that question this way: "The police? In the black community? My God, that's the ultimate enemy! Don't call the police over here; they'll probably beat you up, drag your man off, and throw him in jail for three hundred years!"

Maybe your reaction to that question is similar to Lynn's. The reasons might be different. It all depends on who you are and where you live. For instance, in some rural areas, you may know that police don't take domestic violence seriously.

Make an Informed Decision: See an Advocate

Before you decide what to do, you need information. You need to know about the justice system in your particular town. How likely is it to respect people from your culture or in your situation? The best place to find out about your local law enforcement is from a domestic violence advocate. If you don't know whom to contact in your town, call the National Domestic Violence Hotline, 800/799-SAFE (800/799-7233), or TTY 800/787-3224. Ask for the number of a nearby advocate. Call and ask specific questions. If the advocate doesn't know the answers, she can find them for you. You need information from someone who understands domestic violence *and* your particular situation. She has information about how systems work. *You* are the expert on your own situation. Together the two of you can develop a safety plan.

Questions to Expect and to Ask

A legal domestic violence advocate might ask you these questions:

1. Are you in serious physical danger?
2. Can you get away in an emergency?
3. Are you in a situation (rural, undocumented immigrant, have disabilities, Deaf) that could make it risky to call police?
4. What would you want from police if you did call? Arrest? Referral to a group? A little jail time? A judge to give a "slap on the wrist"?

Here are some questions you might ask the advocate:
1. What are the attitudes of local police, prosecutors, and judges toward women who are abused; toward women in your situation (immigrant, Deaf, etc.); toward men (and women) who batter?
2. What actions have they taken in the past? (Have they arrested victims? Taken women to a shelter? Arrested the abuser?)
3. How likely is it that police will take the action I want from them?
4. Are police attitudes or actions likely to put me in more danger?
5. How long might it take for police to get to my house?
6. Does 911 have a TTY? Will police get a (foreign-language or ASL) interpreter for me when they come?

If You Do Call the Police

We discuss in Chapter 1 the advantages and disadvantages of following most safety plans. If you do decide you'll call the police, practice what to say. Make it clear that it's an emergency, and give your address.

How to Get the Best Response from Police

1. Be as calm as possible.
2. Show them "no contact" or "restraining" orders, if you have them.
3. Tell them about the assault in detail.
4. Show them any injuries, bruises, or damaged property.
5. Don't be afraid to ask the police to make a report.
6. Let them know if anyone saw the attack.
7. Let them know if the man has hit you at other times.
8. Ask for phone numbers of a local domestic violence shelter or hotline.
9. If necessary, ask to be taken to a hospital or safe place.
10. Ask for the case number of the officer's report and a phone number to track the case.

When Might Police Make an Arrest?

Police must have good reason to believe a crime has been committed. They must see some evidence of the crime, such as a bloody nose or other injury. But you can never be sure what the officer will do. Communities differ and so do officers. They might arrest the abuser:

1. *If* your state has a law that police are required to arrest when there is an assault
2. *If* they know about another crime the abuser has committed
3. *If* the assault was serious, involving a weapon or major injury
4. *If* the abuser assaults an officer or an officer sees him attack you

Next Steps

Once you call police, the case might go to court. But it might not. The prosecutor decides that. Prosecutors might ask you what you want. But they often do what they think best regardless of your opinion. If the abuser gets a jail sentence, that can help you be safe. But a prosecutor may not think about what can happen after the abuser gets out of jail. You could then be in more danger. Think carefully about this long before you face an emergency.

The court also can order him to:

- Not contact you for a certain period (called a no-contact order or a temporary restraining order)
- Get treatment for alcoholism or drug abuse
- Pay for your medical treatment
- Replace damaged or stolen property
- Attend a batterers' group. Only a local expert can give you accurate information about this topic. A group could be useful to him. It could also be more dangerous for you. (See the chapter "Men Who Batter: Can They Change?" in *Getting Free*.)

Again, think this through. Have you cooperated in pressing charges before? Did you get the results you wanted? Or did you feel let down or betrayed by the system? If so, you may not want to try it again.

Perhaps the first time you called the police you wanted your partner to go to court. You were scared. You were angry. But as time passed, your feelings changed. You decided you still loved the abuser. The idea of "putting him in jail" made you feel guilty. Maybe you were afraid a jail term would make him furious and more dangerous. Or you needed his financial help. If you believe you will never have to call the police, you might have any one of these second thoughts. But suppose the worst happens and you have no plan to deal with it. You don't know where to go or how to find help. You see only one option. You go back to the abuser. He might try to get you to stop the prosecution. But you can't do that. Only the prosecutor or the judge can stop it.

Find out where you can get help—before you need it. A shelter legal advocate can tell you what to expect in court. Perhaps the justice system has improved since last time. State laws may even have changed. She can help you prepare for an emergency. Later if you are in danger, you can act immediately. You will have a plan in place.

You can also line up a friend to help. She can be in court with you. She might also go with you when you meet with a prosecutor.

Prosecution

If you did call the police, and the prosecutor doesn't take the case to court, ask why. Here are some possible reasons:

- Your injuries do not appear to be serious.
- The abuser says he didn't intend to hurt you.
- You have little or no evidence of assault or injury.
- There is no record of previous assaults or other crimes.
- The prosecutor does not believe you will cooperate.
- The prosecutor is afraid of losing the case.

Success at trial depends on many factors. Here are some:

- How convincing the evidence is
- Whether the judge believes battering is a crime
- How hard the prosecutor works on your case
- Whether batterers' intervention programs are an option
- Whether the abuser seems sorry
- Whether he seems to be a "solid citizen"

Success at trial can be defined differently by you and the prosecutor. For him or her it might mean your partner goes to jail, alcohol or drug treatment, or a batterers' program. (Again, see the chapter "Men Who Batter: Can They Change?" in *Getting Free*.)

Maybe you just want the abuse to stop. That possibility depends on a number of factors:

- The abuser must want to change.
- He must be willing to attend a batterers' group for six months or a year.
- He must be willing to stop all emotional abuse.
- The group must be accredited by the state.
- Group leaders must hold him accountable.
- Group leaders must periodically consult with you on his progress.
- Your partner must be willing to separate if that is what you want.

- He must be willing to go to alcohol or drug counseling if required.
- Your child custody rights must not be at risk.

Your partner might make false promises about what he is willing to do. He might not think there is anything wrong with emotional abuse. He might say that since he is signed up for the group, you have to take him back. Each one of those is a reason to expect him not to change. An advocate can help you decide what is likely to help and what might make things worse.

Your partner may try to gain custody of the children. That can bring up many more issues (see Chapter 15).

Do You Need to Hire Your Own Lawyer?

You may need a lawyer if you are:

- Ending a marriage
- Separating from the father of your children

A lawyer can be very costly. There are some free legal services for abused women. But they are rare. To find out what your community offers, call a domestic violence advocate. You can find one at a shelter or hotline.

Before You See a Lawyer

Ask an advocate to recommend a lawyer who understands abuse. Ask friends and women in support groups for names. Before you see a lawyer, try to decide what you want. It's not a lawyer's job to sort out your emotions. If he or she listens to how you feel, it could cost a lot. You will be charged for the time, even on the telephone.

It is hard to sort out feelings by yourself. A counselor may help. But first, try to answer these questions:

1. Do you want a divorce? This question might be very hard to face. To help think it through, read Chapters 1 through 7 again. Look again at your fears. Will your friends and family stand by you? What about money and support of your children? What other problems are you fearful of? What can you do to make them less difficult?

2. If you want a divorce, is this the right time? Weigh the pros and cons carefully. Make a safety plan for staying and leaving. If you decide to leave, follow it step by step.

3. If you are likely to have a custody struggle, you have many things to consider (see Chapter 15).

Should You See a Counselor?

Women who have been abused face many problems. Some of these are emotional. Chapter 9 discusses ways you can deal with the problems yourself. Friends and family can help, too. Even so, you may want to talk to a professional counselor or therapist.

Your counselor must be someone who understands battering. She must know how much danger you are in. Then she can help you decide whether or not to leave your partner. If you want, she can help you stick to whatever decision you make.

Ask friends, women at support groups, and an advocate for names of good counselors. What did they like about them? What problems were they helpful with?

It is essential that your counselor understand the dynamics of abuse. Ask the counselor what experience she or he has in helping abused women. Ask what she thinks causes abuse. If she says the cause is that the abuser is "sick" or under stress or was abused as a child, she does not understand. (These factors might contribute to abuse. But they do not cause it.) Does she or he believe women are to blame for staying with abusers?

What if you don't like the way the counselor treats you? What if, after a while, you don't think you are making progress? You have the right to tell your counselor. See if you can find a better way to work together. If not, you have a right to leave. There are lots of counselors. Keep trying until you find the one who is right for you.

△

Chapter 9

You Can Be Your Own Counselor

Professionals can be lifesavers. But sooner or later, it's up to you to help yourself.

Right now, you may think that you are the last person you can count on. You feel confused. Depressed. Uncertain of what you want to do. Your will to act seems paralyzed. Sometimes you think you're going crazy.

None of that needs to last forever. You *can* help yourself, even while you're confused. You've already begun—by reading this book. You *can* change the way you think and feel about yourself. That can help you find the strength to act.

Changing the Way You Talk to Yourself

An abused woman gets a lot of verbal abuse. Usually she can't take this for long without being affected. Eventually, she may even believe what's being said about her. She starts saying the same things to herself.

All of us give ourselves messages. We can give ourselves messages that help us. But we can also say things that lead to failure:

"You don't deserve nice clothes. You're too fat and ugly."

"You're helpless and stupid and can't take care of yourself."

"Nothing is ever going to turn out right for you."

If you give yourself messages such as these, your life probably won't get better. You may promise yourself that you'll make changes. But you also go on telling yourself that you're a hopeless mess. If you're hopeless, how can you make your life better?

You can begin by changing the messages you tell yourself. You can't change the abuser, but at least you can stop abusing *yourself!*

What Are You Telling Yourself?

It's important that you put your thoughts on paper. That way, you can *see* your thoughts. Seeing them will help you do something about them. If your thoughts remain silent, you might pretend they aren't there.

List your self-criticisms exactly as you think them: "Dummy!" "Oh my god, you screwed up again!" Some may be single words: "fat," "ugly," "stupid," "hopeless." Others may be whole sentences or paragraphs: "You idiot! You really are a hopeless fool. You ruin everything you touch. You never learn. You keep saying you'll reform, but you won't. You're ugly. You're fat, too, because you don't have any willpower."

Activity 5   *Self-Criticism List*

1. _____

2. _____

3. _____

4. _____

5. _____

6. _____

7. _____

8. _____

9. _____

10. _____

You may talk to yourself this way, silently and often. But it's worse than if another person were saying it to you. Other people speak to you out loud. You know what they are saying, and you can talk back. But if the criticisms are silent, you may never respond to them. The silent messages will continue to tear you down.

Once you know what you're saying to yourself, you can change it.

General Statements and Factual Statements

Many of your self-criticisms are general statements. A general statement is about the kind of person you think you are. An example would be: "You're stupid."

A factual statement is about a particular fact. It may be something you did. Examples would be: "You made a mistake" or "You overslept." It may be about something that happened. For example: "Your car broke down."

The two kinds of statements have very different effects. "You're stupid" leaves no room for change. Compare that with the statement "You made a mistake." This statement allows for the possibility that you are not stupid. You can change the way you act and what you do. Even smart people do stupid things from time to time. Everybody makes mistakes.

If you find yourself being self-critical, take steps to stop it. Here is an example of what one woman does:

1. Accuses herself of being stupid
2. Writes down her thoughts
3. Analyzes the self-criticism and sees that it refers to one fact
4. States what actually happened

Write down your statements. Then replace them with what actually happened.

Activity 6 *Sticking to the Facts*

Self-Critical Statement	What Happened
1. *You're sure stupid!*	*Burned the toast*
2. *Oh my god, you're never going to change. You'll be a fat, useless slob.*	*Ate double ice-cream cone*
3. _____	_____
4. _____	_____
5. _____	_____

A simple statement of "what happened" isn't a statement of blame. It reduces the guilt, anxiety, and depression that go with self-blame.

Doing the exercise can help free you from self-blame. Then you can think clearly about ways to change the things you do.

Do the exercise every day. Replace every general statement with a fact. Keep doing it until you can do it without even trying. After a while, your inner talk will change. It may go like this:

"Well, fatty, you did it again! . . . Whoops, I mean . . . let's see, what did I do? Correction: I had potatoes and gravy."

Before long, you'll be skipping right over the "Well, fatty" remarks. You'll replace them with a simple statement of what you ate.

What Did You Do Right Today?

Abused women often find it hard to think of anything they've done right. How can you get control over your life if you do nothing right? You need to start noticing things that deserve credit.

Here are some things you can take credit for:

Making things better for someone else. Did you listen to someone's troubles? Control your temper with your child? Shop for a sick friend? Prepare a meal? Smile at someone who looked lonely?

Starting to get more control over your life. Did you make a decision? Make a phone call to get information? Begin to learn how to drive or use a computer?

Making yourself feel better. Did you take time to look at the sunset? Walk for the fun of it? Play cards with a good friend? Go out to listen to music?

Make a list of all the things you did right today. They

don't have to be a big deal. When you're feeling low, a small effort is worth a lot.

Suppose you decided today to take up jogging. Maybe you didn't get any farther than one block, but you got up off your chair. You made a step in the direction of change. You deserve credit for that.

Each item you add to your list will strengthen you. The list shows that you've already done some worthwhile things. You'll gain courage to try more of them. You'll begin to get a sense of what is possible.

△

Chapter 10

A Courageous Act a Day

A courageous act is any worthwhile thing you do in spite of being afraid. Worthwhile simply means an activity worth doing. It might be asking a friend to come to dinner. It might be looking for an apartment.

You may think that "little" things such as these aren't courageous acts. You think courage means "big" things, such as saving a drowning person. Yet you may be afraid to do those "little" things yourself. But you don't like to admit it.

Denying Your Fears

It's not strange that you don't like to admit feeling scared. Such feelings are painful. You hope that if you deny having them, they'll go away.

But most of the time, they won't go away. You don't become less anxious by denying the way you feel. You just put off doing whatever it is that makes you feel anxious. It goes like this:

"I shouldn't be nervous about a little thing like

apartment hunting. So I'm *not* nervous. I'm just not doing it today because I think I'm getting a cold. I'll do it tomorrow." And when tomorrow comes, you say, "I couldn't look for an apartment because I missed the bus. I'll go tomorrow."

Those are not reasons. They're excuses. Excuses explain why it's *hard* to do something. They don't explain why you *didn't* do it.

When you keep putting off doing something, listen to your explanations. Are they good reasons for putting it off? Or are they really excuses? Okay, you missed the bus. Why didn't you take the next bus? Don't use this question to blame yourself. Use it to understand what's really going on.

If you're making excuses, you're probably trying to hide your fears from yourself. To find out if that's what you're doing, try this: Ask yourself if you really mean "couldn't." "Couldn't" often means "didn't want to." That often means, "I was too scared, but didn't want to admit it."

If you continue to deny your fears, you can go on putting things off. But when you admit your fears, you can make yourself rise above them. That takes courage. Here are ways you can increase your courage.

Taking the First Steps

Suppose you've been telling yourself you'll go out and get a job. Or you've told yourself you'll rent an apartment or make a new friend. But then you think how you'll feel if you don't get what you want. You're afraid you will feel like a failure. Then you get depressed. So you keep putting it off.

You have put yourself through "failure." And yet you haven't tried!

You need to think about your plans differently. Think only in terms of what you know you can do. "I'm going to *look* for a job or apartment." "I'm going to *invite* someone in for coffee."

This may seem like a small difference, but it is important. You can't control what other people do, but you can control *your* part of the action. If you don't get the job, you don't have to blame yourself. You tried hard. You can give yourself credit for that.

Choose your task with care. Make it one you're willing and able to carry out. Be clear about exactly what you want to do. Afterward, be clear about whether you did it. If you didn't do it at all, did you do some of it? If not, figure out why. Once you know that, you can work on changes. And give yourself credit for the part you *did* do.

Maybe you decided to go to a community college, but you kept putting off applying. You ask yourself why. And you answer that you're afraid you'll flunk out.

It will help if you stop thinking about taking hard courses. There may be easy ones to take first. Sometimes there are even courses for people who have been out of school for years.

Think about the *first* thing you have to do. Maybe you need to talk to a college counselor. If that seems too hard, choose something easier. It might be talking to a friend who's a student. Maybe it's walking through the campus, noticing how many older students there are.

Break the task down into small steps. Choose a first step you *know* you can take. Then take it.

Take Credit for Each Courageous Act

Give yourself credit for the hard things you do. You probably find it easy to tell others they're doing well. You give credit to those around you—husband, lover, children, friends. But you find it hard to take credit for yourself.

Make up your mind to treat yourself well. Don't say, "I don't deserve it." You deserve good treatment, just like anyone else.

Review "What Did You Do Right Today?" in Chapter 9. When you value yourself, others will value you. Start giving yourself rewards.

Be Good to Yourself

Being good to yourself means giving yourself rewards for courageous acts. It also means allowing yourself pleasures for no special reasons. Either way, you have to know what makes you feel good.

See how many pleasures you can think of. Some should be pleasures that are easily available. Maybe you love to listen to music. Start being good to yourself right now, and play your favorite record.

Don't be afraid to plan for bigger pleasures, too. Suppose you want a long vacation by yourself or with another adult. If you have children, that may be an impossible dream for now. But you may be able to go away for a weekend. That would be a start toward your big dream.

It's sometimes painful to be aware of all the things you want. It's hard when you don't have the time or money for them. Yet it's important not to lose sight of what you want. Unless you know what you want, you can't begin to get it.

Find Out What Would Give You Pleasure

On the next page, make three lists:

1. Pleasures you enjoy and want more of
2. Pleasures you used to have (at any time in your life)
3. Things you might like but have never tried (photography, gardening, mystery novels, bowling)

Don't forget small pleasures. Do you like reading in bed? Baking? Taking long walks? Be sure to include those.

Activity 7A *Pleasures List*

Pleasures I Enjoy	Pleasures I Used to Have	Pleasures I Might Like to Have
Watering plants	Riding bikes	Writing poetry
Talking to friends	Sewing	Yoga
_____	_____	_____
_____	_____	_____
_____	_____	_____
_____	_____	_____
_____	_____	_____
_____	_____	_____

Put a check next to pleasures you might have in the next week. Include those for which you need to plan or get information. Be sure there are some you can get right away and that don't cost anything. Do you have at least ten? If not, go back and see what you can add.

Make a list of pleasant events you can look forward to. Include a pleasant event for each part of the day.

Activity 7B   *Daily Pleasures*

Morning	Afternoon	Evening
Watch sunrise	Lunch with coworker	Phone friend
Take a short walk	Window shopping	Cooking
_____	_____	_____
_____	_____	_____
_____	_____	_____
_____	_____	_____
_____	_____	_____
_____	_____	_____
_____	_____	_____

Your list shows that you can have some pleasures in life. You can wake up each morning with things to look forward to.

Diane was surprised to learn how many things she enjoyed doing alone. "I guess I thought I would die from loneliness, but I really don't need somebody to keep me entertained. I've got my books, I've got my stereo . . ."

Take Care of Your Physical Self

It's important to take good care of your body. If you don't feel well, you can feel depressed. It can also make it hard for you to think clearly.

Eat well. Stay away from junk food. If you must have something sweet, buy or fix something really special. Let yourself plan it and enjoy it without feeling guilty. Otherwise, eat what's good for you and enjoy it. Don't eat on the run and don't skip meals.

Sleep well. Try to get about eight hours of sleep each night. If you have trouble sleeping, try to start relaxing an hour before bedtime. If it doesn't work, don't toss and turn. Pass the time enjoyably: Listen to soothing music or read something light. Stretch and rest without trying to sleep.

Don't panic if you're not getting a regular good night's sleep. You won't fall apart. Don't tell yourself, "I've got to sleep tonight or I'll be a mess tomorrow." That will make it even harder to relax and sleep.

If you feel tired most of the time, see a doctor. If you get sleeping pills, don't use them for more than a month. A doctor might not tell you whether the pills are addictive. They can also have dangerous side effects. Drinking alcohol to fall asleep can be a dangerous habit, too.

Exercise. Exercise will make you feel and look better. Concentrate on the pleasure of moving your body. If you're out of shape, start slowly. Stay with it only as long as it feels good. If you stop while you're enjoying it, you'll probably do it again. It will help you to make exercise a regular part of your life.

Look good. The way you look affects the way you feel. Don't give yourself a chance to feel sloppy. Fix your hair and put on whatever makeup you usually wear. Do these things even if you're not leaving the house or seeing anyone. It's a way of reminding yourself that *you* care about you.

Chapter 11

△

Steps to Finding Friends

Abusive men often demand that their partners give up other relationships. So, by now, you may have few or no friends.

You may think that friends can't give you much, compared with a lover. It's true that there are differences between what each can give. But some of the differences exist only in our minds. We *think* that only sexual relationships can be intimate and caring, so we place limits on what to expect of friends. We can change that attitude if we want to.

Lynn has advice for women who have been isolated by abusive men: "When you feel lonely, instead of looking for a man, you can go with some women to hear music. . . . If I hadn't left, I wouldn't have known all these great women."

Why Aren't Acquaintances Friends?

Often, women don't see the flaws in people they hope will become lovers. Yet they find many things "wrong" with people who might become friends. You can change the way you look at people who might become friends.

A lonely person may find fault with everyone. She may feel that nobody would want her for a friend. So she rejects people before they have a chance to reject her.

Is this something you do? To find out, list several people you see from time to time. Include people you work with or see in the neighborhood. Include those you see at church, at school, and where you do your shopping. Include relatives and former friends. Add the reason she is not a close friend.

Activity 8 *Why Aren't Acquaintances Friends?*

1. Mary   *Sister-in-law; lives in another city*

2. Betty   *Neighbor; gossips too much*

3. _____

4. _____

5. _____

6. _____

7. _____

8. _____

9. _____

Do you think some of these people might become friends? If so, you have a good pool to draw from. If not, you have a problem to solve. Did you mostly write down things you don't like about the people? If so, notice whether you wrote general statements, such as "stupid," "nosy," or "a fool."

If you did that, you might want to change the pattern. Turn back to Activity 6 in Chapter 9. Follow the same method to replace the statements above. Change general statements to facts. "She's a fool" will become "She giggles when she's nervous." Practice this method. After a while, the put-downs will be replaced by simple descriptions. Then you can decide whether the person's flaws are really important.

Don't pass up a chance at a friendship by being too critical. Take a chance with a few people. If you spend a little time with them, you might be less lonely. Pay attention to how you feel about yourself when you're with them. If they make you feel bad, try someone else.

Find people you can enjoy talking with over a cup of coffee. Or someone you'll spend half an hour with after a movie or bowling. She needn't be someone you think will become your best friend. But you need to start someplace. It takes time to make friends. And you can't always tell at first who you'll like.

After a while, some acquaintances will become good friends. Then, if you meet a new man, you can take it slow. You won't feel you *have* to have a man. You'll have friends to be with—friends who care about you. Romance can then be something you *want*. It won't be something you'll die without. Your judgments about the men you become involved with can then become clearer.

Meeting New People

Start looking at everyone you meet as a possible friend. Even if you don't go many places, you meet a lot of people. You meet them at the grocery store or the launderette. You see them in the waiting room of your doctor's or dentist's offices. Have you ever heard of anyone meeting an interesting man in such situations? Why not an interesting woman?

There are even easier places to find friends. Two of the best are classes and volunteer groups. Your job is another.

Classes, Jobs, and Volunteer Groups

Perhaps you need to learn some skills for a job. Or you need to pass a course to get into college. Taking a class may be important to your long-range plans. But classes also give you a chance to meet new people. Think about taking classes where you might find friends.

Look into all-women's classes. At least some of the women will also be there to find friends. And none of you will be trying to impress male classmates. You might want to start with a support group. The YWCA, the National Organization for Women, and some churches offer these.

At most colleges, you will find a women's center. This is a good place to meet people and to get useful information. Find out about classes that are small and informal. They're better places for meeting people than big lecture courses.

If you're job hunting, pay attention to the people you'd be working with. Try to choose a workplace where you think you can find friends. If you're forty, you may feel isolated among workers in their twenties. The same goes for a five-person office where you're the only nonprofessional. Even so, you might meet people who could become friends. It depends on how open you are to different kinds of people.

If you have any extra time, do volunteer work. You'll meet people who care about the same things you do. Watch the newspaper for notices of where volunteers are needed. Or call United Way for the names of groups that want volunteers.

Look at every part of your life in terms of finding friends. You can end your isolation. If you're willing to use some thought and energy, you'll find the way.

Chapter 12

△

Reaching Out

So there you are. You're at the launderette, on the job, or in a class. How do you make a new friend?

Risking the First Steps

To make friends, you must be willing to make the first move. That may be very hard. Why? Because you fear your friendly move may be rejected. But will the sky really fall down if that happens?

Suppose you say something friendly, and the other person turns away. You might feel bad. But that feeling doesn't have to last. You can put it out of your mind. And if the other person *is* friendly, you might make a friend. Isn't it worth the risk?

Getting to Know People on the Job

Suppose you're new on the job. Hardly anybody has spoken to you. You might think that's because nobody's interested in you. But have you done anything to let people know you're interested in *them?* You know you're shy, but they may think you're just unfriendly. You may need to start smiling, to start saying "hello."

If you haven't been friendly so far, they may not smile back at first. It may take several tries before they'll risk being friendly to you. Don't give up if your friendly action is rejected by one person. How do you know they're *all* that way? Is it *all* of them or just one? List the proof you have that *all* of them are unfriendly. Make another list of each friendly gesture you've made to each person.

Make these lists regularly. Make them whenever you think people aren't being friendly to you. It doesn't have to be only the people where you work. Use the lists for other people, too.

Now you have a truer picture of the facts. You can begin to take some risks. Start with things you're sure you can do. You might decide to say good morning to two people at work or give the person at the next desk a compliment.

Build on your success. Try something a little harder. For example, you might talk with someone for ten minutes at lunch next time. Remember that success means doing what you promised yourself to do each day. It has nothing to do with how other people respond to you. You have no control over that.

Activity 9 *Making Friends Checklist*

Why I Think They Don't Like Me	Friendly Gestures I Have Made
1. *Office workers—don't ask me to lunch*	*Said hello to some of them in the elevator*
2. *New neighbors—haven't said hello.*	*None*
3. _____	_____
4. _____	_____
5. _____	_____
6. _____	_____

Getting to Know People in Classes and Organizations

You spend less time with people in classes and groups than at work. So you'll have to move a little faster to make friends. If you delay, the whole activity might be over before you get started.

How to Begin

A perfect time for informal, friendly talk is before classes or meetings start. Arrange to arrive ten minutes early. You'll be one of the first to meet people, to learn their names. This will make you feel more secure before the group starts. It will help you risk being more outgoing.

In a classroom or meeting, look around. Listen. Decide who you're interested in getting to know. Be ready to introduce yourself when there's a break. It's sometimes hard just to cross a room. But do it anyway.

A few friendly words will start you off. "How long have you been volunteering here?" "Have you taken classes here before?"

Following Up

If all goes well, you'll have a pleasant talk. Say a word or two again before you leave, such as, "I enjoyed talking with you. See you next week." If you want to be very brave, you might offer the person a ride next week. Or ask her for one.

She may say, "Thanks, but I'm coming from another direction." Don't assume that's a brush-off. She may think it's only a ride you want, not friendship. Make another friendly attempt. If she still doesn't respond, try someone else you think you might like.

Some people you speak to may not have time for a new friend. Don't let that make you feel you're not worth knowing. If you are easily hurt, though, play it safe. Begin by trying to find friends among women who are new in town or those who are newly separated from mates.

> Joan found a good friend in Parents Without Partners. But it was hard at first. "The first time I went to a Parents Without Partners meeting, I was petrified. But I wasn't expected to do anything, and I could just sit there and observe, so I felt safe. . . . Then I met another woman, and we decided to go to the meetings together."

Getting Help from Your Family

Family members don't always support you. Maybe you kept your abuse a secret from them before. So it may be hard for them to believe you now. They may blame you for leaving your man. They may need time to get used to the truth.

On the other hand, perhaps family members knew about the abuse all along. They may have urged you to leave and blamed you when you didn't. Now they expect you to be happy right away. They get impatient or angry with you if you're lonely sometimes. They're afraid you'll go back to him.

Try to explain your feelings to your family. If they go on being negative, protect yourself. Avoid discussions that upset you. Stop seeing family members who make you feel bad. You don't have to make a lot of excuses. You can just say you feel better when you spend more time alone.

Ask your family to learn about battering in books or TV programs. Check in to see if their ideas have changed. Don't give up on them. They may do things that upset you *because* they care about you.

Dealing with Kindness

Families who really want to help can also be a problem. They can try too hard to protect you.

Maybe you've gone to your parents' house. You plan to stay a day or two. But they want you to move in for good. You know it's time to find a place of your own. But it's also comforting and easier to stay with them. So you don't even look at apartment ads.

Such kindness can make you feel helpless. If you see that happening, speak up. Tell your family you need help in becoming independent. That's the best kind of support they can give you.

Chapter 13

△

The First Week

Your first week on your own may be difficult. Where and how you spend it is important.

Staying in a Shelter for Battered Women

A battered women's shelter can be helpful. You'll find people there who understand why you left. They'll help you stay away from your partner, if that's what you want. The shelter may have a secret address and phone number. If so, your man won't be able to find you.

Leaving home is hard. You'll be worried about money, child care, work, or school. Shelter workers will help you sort out your problems. You'll meet other women in situations like yours. Talking with them can make your loneliness and fears easier to handle.

Melissa tried to stay with friends. But her violent boyfriend found out where she was. At last, she went to a battered women's shelter. "I was frightened when I got there, but they were great, so supportive, and everyone helped. Everyone shared stories about how they coped. Everyone had basically the same story. . . . It still gives me goosebumps to remember the closeness and support I felt there."

Safe Homes

Safe Homes are often available in small towns where there are no shelters. Safe Homes are also in large cities. You will probably be the only guest staying there. A Safe Home is someone's private house. The people who live there give shelter to battered women and their children. It may be for only a few days. But in those few days, you will be well cared for. And you will experience life in a nonabusive family.

Don't wait until you're in immediate danger. This is a good time to gather information. You can phone the toll-free National Domestic Violence Hotline at 800/799-SAFE (800/799-7233), or TTY 800/787-3224. An advocate there can tell you how to reach the nearest shelter or Safe Home.

Staying with Friends or Relatives

It's a comfort to stay with someone who cares about you. Also, there may be no time limit on how long you can stay. And with a close friend, you can let out your feelings.

But there are disadvantages, too. It's good for you to let out your feelings sometimes, but it can also encourage you to tell your story over and over. That might be hard for your friend to take. Or it could make her think she should run your life.

It's best to tell your friend or family member clearly what you want. And then ask your host to set limits. If you want advice, ask for it. If you want to be left alone, say so. "I might want to hear some advice in a couple of days. But for now, I'd just like to talk about how I feel. Do you mind just listening? And would you tell me when you've had enough?"

Accept help when you really need it. Don't apologize for accepting it. A simple "thank you" is enough. Let your mother babysit while you go to the lawyer or counselor. Borrow your friend's car to look for permanent housing. Just be sure you've both agreed on what's okay. When in doubt, ask.

Staying Alone

You may decide to live alone. It could be in a new place, or it could be in the home you shared with your partner.

Perhaps you're fairly sure the abuser won't come after you. Even so, it's a good idea to change door locks. Put locks on the windows, too. Although it may seem embarrassing, tell new or old neighbors what's going on. Ask them to call you or the police if they hear sounds of violence. A little embarrassment may mean the difference between life and death.

When you live alone, you have to work hard to not be lonely. Get in touch with friends, relatives, a counselor, or a support group. (Review Chapters 11 and 12.) Make a list of crisis line numbers. Keep the list by your telephone. Don't wait until you're desperate to use it.

It will help you to go to a support group for abused women. Many shelters have these groups. Shelters can also give you information about other support groups in your community.

Contact with the Abuser

If you have left your partner, you probably thought about the decision long and hard. You decided you had to leave to be safe. "Safe" includes your feelings about yourself as well as physical safety. It is important to feel confident and worthwhile. If you don't, it can be very hard to take good care of yourself. Your ex-partner has probably not changed. He may become even more violent after you leave. That could happen even if he "only" humiliated and controlled you in the past. Unless he has attended a batterers' intervention group for several months, he is not safe for you.

Even if he has, you should ask his group leader about his progress. You need to be careful not to fool yourself into thinking it is safe to be with him.

You can give yourself lots of reasons to call the man you left. But wait. Don't do it. Give yourself the same advice you'd give an alcoholic about having just one drink. It's not worth the risk.

For the first week, try to follow two rules:

1. Don't see the abuser, no matter what.

2. Don't talk to him on the phone, no matter what.

These rules may seem easy the first few days after you've left. You may be able to both see and feel your injuries. You may think you never want to see your abuser again. But sometime during the first or second week, these feelings may change. You may begin to remember happy times with him.

This is an important time. Get ready for it. Here's how.

Most Dangerous List

Make a list of the worst things your partner has done to you. Include every pain and humiliation. These things are dangerous to your physical and mental health. Include the things he said to you afterward, whether cruel or loving. You're probably going to hear those "loving" promises again. This sheet will help you remember how little they meant.

Maybe you think you'll never forget the terrible things he's done. But remember the last time you took him back? Didn't you forget then? Write it all down whether you believe you can forget or not. It will be painful. But it could save your life.

Activity 10 *Most Dangerous List*

1. _____

2. _____

3. _____

4. _____

5. _____

6. _____

7. _____

8. _____

9. _____

Best Memories List

Now make a list of the good things your partner has done for you. Include happy moments and the hopes and dreams you shared. Add things you like or admire about your partner.

Activity 11   *Best Memories List*

1. _____
2. _____
3. _____
4. _____
5. _____
6. _____
7. _____
8. _____
9. _____

Compare the lists. Relive your feelings during good times and bad. Were the good things worth the bad ones?

Change List

"We could be so happy if only he would . . ." Make a list of the most important "if onlys." What things would he *have* to change for you to risk going back? A sample list might include:

- Never hit me, no matter what I do.
- Don't insult me or make fun of me.

- Go to a batterers' group for at least six months.
- Go to AA for at least six months.
- Don't try to stop me if I want to see friends, get a job, etc.
- Give me a certain sum of money monthly, and we decide on the amount together. No questions to be asked about how I spend it.

Activity 12 *Change List*

1. _____
2. _____
3. _____
4. _____
5. _____
6. _____
7. _____
8. _____
9. _____

Put a check mark next to any changes he said he'd make in the past but didn't. Also put a check mark next to those he has refused to discuss with you. Have you any reason to believe things will be different in the future? Has he started to make big changes on any item listed?

If he has started to make some changes, that's good. But wait a while. See how long they last. Is it safe to go back to him because he promised? Or because he said he called a counselor? Or even if he went to a counselor one time?

It's easy for him to promise. The real test is whether he follows through. It will be months before you can be sure.

Using the Lists

Read the lists any time you're tempted to call or see the abuser. Read the Most Dangerous List aloud. Force yourself to live through the abuse again in your mind. Always keep the list near you. You'll be able to read it any time you feel weak. It can stop you from getting in touch with him.

Read the Best Memories List, too. You can look at both the good and the bad, and think:

"Yes, he can be sweet. He gave me roses, he was fun. But those times can never make up for the others. Like the miscarriage he caused the day he knocked me down the stairs."

Read your Change List. Check the items he's actually changed and for how long. Compare what's actually happened with what the list demands. The answer to what you should do will be right there.

Chapter 14

△

Nurturing Your Children: Safety and Resilience

You can help your children become strong, loving people. You can teach them to protect themselves. Teach them to break self-destructive habits. Let them know the abuse is not their fault. Show them they are good, competent, useful people, able to solve problems. To be "resilient" means that they are confident, that they believe they can take care of themselves. It means they appreciate their own abilities. Children may be abused either directly or by observing violence. In either case what they most need is one adult they can trust. This chapter offers ideas about how you can be that trusted adult.

Safety Whether You Leave or Stay

To reduce the harm of abuse, first increase your children's safety. You might get a lot of advice from social workers. They try hard to help. So might friends and family. Often they do help. But sometimes they don't know enough about abuse. Maybe they insist that you leave the abuser right away. They say you must do that "for the sake of the children." But they may not know it can be more dangerous to leave than to stay. Many don't know that if you do leave, you have to plan carefully.

In the long run it might be safer if you leave. But timing is important. Here are some of the most dangerous times:

- When you just told the abusive person you are going to leave
- When you have just moved out
- When he has just been served with divorce papers
- When the court has changed his visiting rights

Some abused women have even been killed during such periods. Maybe they didn't plan for safety carefully enough. Others might have made fine plans but couldn't carry them out.

Those facts are not an argument for staying with the abuser. They are reminders: If you leave, you need to plan carefully. You need to do it in the safest way. Weigh the risks at each step. Even if you plan to leave, you may not do it right away. It will take time to gather important documents and supplies. For now, focus on how to increase your safety for whatever period you stay with the abuser.

▲ △ ▲

Start Safety Planning Now

You might want to stay. But what if your partner chokes you or threatens you with a gun? You might be forced to leave. Plan for the worst. Decide now how you will get out of the house. How will you protect your children? Where will you go? How will you get there? You might stay in a safe place for a few hours or a few days.

This is a good time to review Chapter 1. At each step of our suggested safety plans consider alternatives. What is the likelihood of danger and safety for each one? Weigh that against *not* taking each step. Then make a decision. Maybe it will work out well. If it doesn't, adjust it. Show your kids it's important not to give up.

Helping Your Children Be Safer at Home

Include your children in your safety plans. Help them make their own plans. Tell them what arrangements you have made for security at work. Use the ideas on the next page and the ideas in Chapter 1 to create a plan that suits you.

Your children should know that plans are essential. But explain that they don't always work. If that happens, it's not anyone's fault. If there are problems, you try something different. Things might change at the last minute. It might not be possible to follow the plan. Explain that the kids are not to blame if they cannot get away or call for help.

Activity 13 *Steps for Safety Planning at Home*

> 1. Ask the children to name someone they would turn to for help in a dangerous situation.
>
> 2. Find out if they would ask that person for help.
>
> 3. If not, talk with them about their reasons.
>
> 4. Talk to that person about your plan.

Help Your Child Identify Warning Signs

Talk to your children about what their father does that hurts you or them. Do not say he is a terrible person. "Sometimes your dad acts in ways that are scary. Then we need to do things to try to stay safe." Here are examples:

- Mom and Dad are arguing.
- Dad is raising his voice.
- Dad or Mom is drunk or high.
- Dad is name-calling or threatening.
- Dad is slamming doors or stomping around.

How Kids Can Increase Their Safety

Let your children know what they should do if the above warning signs occur:

- Go to their rooms.

- Leave the house for somewhere safe. Go to a neighbor's or relative's house. Go outside—if the neighborhood is safe.
- Stay out of the way.
- Try to get to a room where there is a phone.
- Know how to dial 911. Try to get to a phone where the abuser can't hear.
- Stay away from the kitchen and bathroom.
- Do not try to stop the violence.

How Violence Affects Children

You might be tempted to tell the children that nothing happened. "It was just a bad dream." Many children blame themselves for a parent's violence. Often the abuser tells them it is their fault. It is your job to help them understand that "Yes, it happened," and "No, it is not your fault." They might worry about you, too. You may want to say everything is fine. But they know everything is not fine, and your denial will confuse them. It can reduce their trust in you. They need to hear the truth. "It happened. It hurts. It is not your fault." They may need to hear it over and over. They need to know they can count on you to tell them the truth. And to care for them. And to let them talk about their feelings.

The Children Who "Only" Observe Battering

"They're asleep; they never hear it," you say.

"They're too young to understand; they don't
know it's happening," he says.

Most children interviewed after their mothers were assaulted say they knew what was happening. They saw and heard much more than their parents thought they did. Many suffered from what they observed. They were lonely, slept poorly, or did not eat well. They felt depressed, had headaches, or could not keep frightening thoughts away. Some identified with the violent partner. They became aggressively angry. They bullied other children or even their mothers.

Promoting Resiliency in the Midst of Chaos

Your children might suffer from any of those reactions. But that does not mean you can't help them change. You are the most important person in their lives. You can help them develop ways to cope and recover. Protect them. Fight for their rights. You can become a positive influence on them. You can do that even while you are still living with the abuser.

Anita put herself between her son and his violent

father. That kept her son from being beaten and let him know how much she cared.

Maybe you feel guilty about how the abuse affects your children. But you are *not* responsible for what your partner does. You *are* responsible for trying to protect the kids. And you have probably tried hard to do exactly that. Another tough job is to keep a positive attitude. You can do that even when your life is frightening. Help your children focus on the things they can control. Their own pattern of thinking is one of those.

You can model ways to look positively at what has happened. "Terrible things have happened to us. But we can cope." Activities 5 and 6 in Chapter 9 and 7A and 7B in Chapter 10 show you how to control your thinking. Help your children do those same activities. Help them notice the negative comments they make. Encourage them to substitute neutral ones.

An Anxious and Clinging Child

Suppose your six-year-old child, Maria, is timid and anxious. Her whining drives you crazy. That might be her way of saying, "Please pay attention. I'm scared."

Maybe you're scared too, or feel too exhausted to take good care of Maria. But you are the one she counts on. So begin with whatever you can manage. Read to her or play

with her—do *something* with her—even if it's for five minutes. Don't answer the phone or sneak looks at the televi-
sion. Your full attention tells her you care about her.

When she does something well, tell her you've noticed.
Help her bake cookies or plant flowers. Let her know you
have confidence in her. She will begin to realize she can
predict and control some aspects of her life. She will have
a good chance of becoming a resilient child.

An Angry Child

Let's say Maria's twelve-year-old brother copies your husband's abuse. He insults you and hits his sister. He refuses
to admit he feels sad or helpless. You might forget that he
is hurting too.

Let him know it's okay to feel sad and angry. But insist
he stick to the rules you make. Even if he won't admit it, he
needs to be cared for. But take it slow. Give him time and
attention without criticism. Try watching a sports TV program with him. If he follows football plays that are confusing to you, ask him to explain. Tell him you think he's
smart for being able to understand the game. Whenever
you notice a skill he's developed, say so. Let him know you
will help him be strong and competent. Encourage activities that enable him to learn new skills. He will begin to
develop self-confidence.

Helping Children Who Have Witnessed Violence

You can take a number of steps to help your children.

- When they are ready, talk with them about the violence.
- Accept that they may not be willing or able to talk about it right away.
- Listen to them.
- Encourage them to talk about their feelings. Help them express them in constructive ways.
- Show understanding.
- Let them know the abuse is not their fault.
- Let them know you love them.
- Let them know by words and actions that you will try to keep them safe.
- Let them know you will help them act in ways that are safe.
- Let them know violence is not okay.
- Acknowledge that it's hard and scary to live through violence.
- Avoid using threats or violence.
- Take them to counseling if they need it.
- Set limits respectfully when your child acts in aggressive, abusive, or violent ways.
- Give your child plenty of time to adapt to the new nonviolent atmosphere you're creating.

(Adapted from *Helping Children Who Witness Domestic Violence: A Guide for Parents (Student Workbook)*, 1997, by Meg Crager and Lily Anderson at www.mincava.umn .edu/documents/materials/study.doc.)

When the Abuser Dominates the Household

Suppose you are living with an abuser. Everything centers on avoiding his violence. It might seem impossible to create a positive environment for the kids. But you can try to schedule activities with your children while the abuser is out. When the children first come home from school, help them fix a special snack. Listen to them talk about their day. Ask what they want to do during the rest of the afternoon. Ask them to think of activities you can do together every day.

Maybe you and your partner get home from work about the same time. But maybe you can get away to the store with the kids. Once there, teach the children how to solve problems. Show them how to choose low-cost nutritious food. The ability to solve problems builds confidence and a sense of being in control. That is the path to resilience. But the main goal at the store is to have a good time together. Make it a little adventure.

At bedtime read a story to them. Or just talk over their day together. Do that even if they are older. Ten minutes they can count on every night can make a difference. Think of activities with the kids that your husband won't want to join. Maybe cooking or gardening. With a bit of thought, you can find something. It takes time to learn a new routine, so try to be patient.

Nurturing the Children If You Leave

If you decide to leave, you might worry about how you will take care of your kids on your own. Many women fear they will never make enough money to support their kids. Yet once they have left, they find better jobs than expected. Or they learn to get along on less. It may take several years to adapt. But being safer and knowing the children are safer can make up for a lower standard of living.

You might even fear that you are beginning to abuse the children yourself. That is a serious worry. But staying with an abusive person won't solve that problem. You can probably be a better parent if you separate. It might be harder at first to cope with your children by yourself. *But most women become better parents by six months after leaving an abuser.*

After you leave, some children will still blame themselves for the abuser's absence or his violence. Or they may have other problems. If so, you might want to get help from a children's counselor. It's often easier for a child to talk to a counselor than to a parent. Try to find a counselor who works with children of abusers. Most shelters can give you this information.

The Value of Mistakes

You and your kids can use your mistakes to figure out what to do better. You have probably tried many ways to protect your children. Maybe some worked for a while and then didn't the next time. The challenge is to bounce back and try something else.

You are not trying to make everything just right. After all, life is full of problems and obstacles. But you can encourage a positive attitude in your children: "I can solve this problem. If this doesn't work, I can try something else."

Keep reminding yourself and your kids of what you are working toward. Your aim is to become a peaceful family. That starts with each person. Maybe your partner refuses to make that a goal. You can still do it on your own, whether you are living with him or not. You can encourage everyone to act in fair and respectful ways. Then help the children take credit for doing that. You are creating a family that is not just free of abuse. It is a home that fosters nonviolence and equal treatment of everyone.

Chapter 15

△

Child Custody and Visitations

To many of us, the legal system is like a foreign land. But guides can help you find the best paths to your goals. They can give you ideas about how to approach a court social worker. They can refer you to the best kind of lawyer. Some of those helpers are friends who will listen to your fears. They might go with you to the social worker or lawyer or courthouse. This chapter doesn't give you legal advice. It suggests ways to approach the professionals you will meet in a custody struggle.

A time may come when you seem to be up against a legal wall. You wonder, "Is it time to accept what I can't change?" Friends will talk you through those periods. Family members, clergy, advocates, and others may also be there for you. So try not to freeze with fear. If you recently left the abuser, you might be sharing child care without a court order. If you get stuck in court before you're ready, a judge may order that you continue those custody arrangements. So as soon as possible, start preparing for a possible legal struggle.

Struggling Against "Court Abuse"

It is worth repeating: "An abuser will use anything he can to gain control of you." He will use the children against you. He might lie about the kind of mother you've been. Suppose you don't speak English or you have a disability? You have not been able to hold a job. You once slapped your child. He might use any of those things to gain custody. If he has money or connections, he will use them. If you are ready for those tactics, you can fight them. You will be prepared to contradict predictable lies. To answer true criticisms, you can say, "Yes, I did that. I've taken action to change it." But it won't help to dwell on your flaws. That is exactly what he hopes you will do.

Taking Control of Your Decisions

Suppose you do have a habit that has negative consequences. Maybe you've used alcohol to take away the pain and fear. There is no point in being angry at yourself. It won't help to worry about how the abuser might use it against you. Focus, instead, on change. Start by attending an AA program right away, even if you change to another program later. Beginning to change now will be good for you and the kids. It can also make a difference in court.

Maybe you really did slap your child. Maybe more than once. It can be useful to remember that it was the wrong thing to do. But telling yourself you're a bad mother won't help. Instead, take action. Enroll in a parenting class. Talk about it to women in a support group. Do whatever it takes to start improving your life. You can establish yourself as a good parent. You can prove to yourself and your kids that a new life is starting.

The abuser might say he's going to keep you in court sessions until you're broke. He could be telling the truth or he could be bluffing. The struggle may be long and hard. But if you decide you want custody, you can get a support team together and fight for it. With that and a good lawyer, you have a good chance of winning. You might be so worn down you think it would be better to try for it later. But you might have trouble being taken seriously later. If you try but don't win, you will feel better about having done as much as you could. And it will be a message to your children that you cared enough to struggle for custody. A long court battle can be as wearing as other kinds of abuse. But this time you can control your own decisions about it.

Create a Support Team

Don't rush into court. You will probably need a lawyer, and finding the best one takes time. Other important actions come first. You can use all the help you can get for emotional support and to brainstorm ideas. If you have been isolated, now is the time to change that.

Enlist the support of family and friends. Consider asking religious leaders. You might also see if your child's teacher will be on your team. Ask help from anyone who knows your situation and cares about you and your kids. If you haven't told them about the abuse, do it now. Explain your feelings and problems to people who want to understand. They can help you clarify your most important goals. It will be good to discuss them with a domestic violence legal advocate. This is your support team.

Add a specialist in any field that affects your specific custody questions. You might need an expert who knows about disability or immigration law or lesbian gay legal issues.

It is usually hard to remember all the important points from meetings. So see if one person can go with you to most of your appointments. Before each meeting, discuss with her what you hope to accomplish. Ask her to help you stay on track. She can gently remind you of your goal by asking, "Were you going to ask about . . . ?" Ask her to take notes, especially when you meet with an "expert."

Members of your support team can brainstorm with you about the best way to approach professionals. They can list what you tell them are your most important points. Then when you go to a meeting, you can refer to that list. For instance, you might be tempted to describe every kind of abuse you endured. But you probably won't have time. Your support person can help you focus on the essential points. Afterward you can discuss the interview. That will help you be clear on what the expert asked you and how you responded. You can record anything you've been asked to do and expectations of what will happen.

Social Workers

Your custody case will center on who is a fit parent. To help the court decide, you may be interviewed by a guardian *ad litem* (GAL) or court-appointed special advocate (CASA). She is likely to be a social worker, so that is the term we use. She could work for the court or for a child-protection agency. Images of having your children instantly taken away may rush through your mind. But that rarely happens. You and the social worker both want to protect the children. You are on the same side. Try to work with her. Be ready to go more than halfway.

Making the Most of an Interview

A social worker might have trouble understanding your situation. You might have to help her. Until recently almost no one understood that domestic abuse existed. That has changed dramatically. But education of the public and professionals takes time. Research tells us that children are harmed by witnessing their mother being abused. But the social worker may not know that. You, your lawyer, or a domestic violence advocate might help explain that. You can tactfully suggest she read Lundy Bancroft and Jay Silverman's book *The Batterer as Parent* or see Bancroft's website for short articles (see the Resources section). Don't imply that she doesn't know her job. Assume she is as interested in protecting your children as you are.

The information about harm to children could backfire, so be prepared. The social worker might say, "Well, if it hurts the child, why haven't you left earlier?" She may believe you have "failed to protect" the children. Tell her calmly what you did to protect them. Explain what is different now. If you did leave earlier and the abuser attacked or stalked you, say that. Help her understand that leaving might have been as risky as staying. You will have to be patient in describing the circumstances. You may have to explain other actions that were hard choices between two bad options.

Explain that you will do whatever is necessary to keep your kids safe. Ask her advice: "My goal is to do everything I can to protect my kids. I'd be glad to explain how I've tried to do that. Please help me with your ideas."

The abuser might try to persuade the social worker that he is the better parent. You can suggest questions for her to ask him. When questioned, some abusive men admit violence to or neglect of a child. They might admit to hitting a child "for his own good." They might not know basic things, such as what grade a child is in.

You can also ask the social worker to interview your child's teacher, your neighbor, or friends. She can ask them about the kind of parent you are. She can find out whether your husband has been closely involved with your child. Be wary, though. If your husband is a clever liar, any of these interviews can go against you if the social worker believes him.

Maybe you have done things you feel guilty about. If so, don't try to hide them. It's true they can look like character flaws. She might believe you won't change. So it may be a risk to tell her. But it's a bigger risk to deny the truth. Describe exactly what you are doing to change. Explain that many women improve their parenting after leaving abusers.

The Attorney
Finding the Right One
Many shelters have legal advocates. They will not act as your lawyer. But they can help you understand what to

expect from the courts. A major challenge is to find a lawyer you can afford. Ask an advocate about free legal services in your area, although fewer are available than before.

Hiring the best lawyer can make a world of difference. The lawyer must understand domestic violence. That includes the dynamics of abuse. It means knowing why women are afraid to leave abusers. It means recognizing how abused women's lives are controlled. It includes knowing how abuse affects children.

Your husband might insist on a court battle. He may have the money for it. He can harass you with "court abuse" for months or years. It may be clear to you that he doesn't care about your children. But a judge or court social worker may not realize he is using the courts to harass you. They may not be prepared to evaluate batterers. Your lawyer should expect that and be prepared to deal with it.

The lawyer should also know the court personnel. That is especially important in rural areas. The judge, police officer, or prosecutor may be your husband's relative. The attorney must also understand other laws that affect your situation. She or he might need expertise in immigration or disability law, for instance. If you have a disability, the abuser will use that against you. He might try to persuade a judge that you can't care for your child.

The judge may not realize that a woman who uses a wheelchair is perfectly able to care for a child.

Probably your illness or disability does not interfere with your caretaking. It might mean you need certain kinds of readily available support. Explain to the social worker your plan for caring for your children. Your lawyer should also understand the law regarding ADA (Americans with Disabilities Act) and what you are capable of. If you will need the support of technical devices or people, try to line it up before you see a social worker. A carefully laid-out plan to care for your children can give you confidence. If you go to court, you can describe it precisely to the judge. If you have no way of financially supporting children, start applying for a job now. Be sure the lawyer knows that is part of your plan.

It is important to consider all these factors before you hire a lawyer. If later you discover your lawyer's lack of expertise, you could change to another attorney, but it is hard to start over with someone new.

Before You See a Lawyer

Try hard to sort out how you feel and what you want. Do that before you see the lawyer. He or she may be willing to listen and advise you on your decisions. But a lawyer is not a trained counselor. And you will almost surely be charged high legal fees for every minute of consultation. That probably includes phone calls. You can go over exactly what you want the lawyer to know with your support team.

Visitations

Try to have your husband's visits supervised. Supervised visits can increase your safety and your children's. You will need a judge's order for that. A good lawyer might be able to make that happen. She or he must understand how an abuser can manipulate the legal system and the children. It may be difficult to persuade a judge that your children's father is a danger to them as well as to you. Your lawyer will know whether it is wise to try. Most likely one of you will have custody and the other visitation rights.

You may already find it difficult to stay away from the abuser. You might still be emotionally attached. Or he may play on your guilt feelings. His visits can create risks of violence. But it is not necessary to see him when one of you visits the children. You can arrange for him to pick them up at a friend's, neighbor's, or relative's house. You can hire a babysitter, even if it's hard to afford. Some cities have special places where children can be transferred without the parents meeting face to face.

No matter how complicated it is, try hard to avoid being with the abuser, especially alone with him. That is especially important right after you separate, when violence is still a serious possibility. You could be in more danger than you were before you left. The first year is the most dangerous time. The first thirty days are especially so. There is no guarantee you will be safe after a year. So don't relax your guard. Your safety plan may change along with different circumstances. But it is important to keep a plan in place.

When Your Children's Father Has Unsupervised Visitation

Ask your lawyer to write a plan that sets out specific requirements for visits. It should include exact details about location, time, and days. Spell out arrangements for the safe transfer of the child. It might require that your ex not drink before or during a visit. Then follow the requirements yourself. Ask a friend or relative to be with you when the children are picked up and returned. Be sure it is someone who understands the abuse. These guidelines are adapted from the Crager and Anderson curriculum:

- Be consistent. Don't let the abuser manipulate or threaten you. Don't change visitation plans to please him. Or for your convenience.
- Don't argue with him about visitation. If he insists, hang up the phone or leave.

- He might say, "Just this time won't hurt." But it might very well hurt. If you give in to him once, he will keep after you to do it again.
- Try to make your child's experience as positive as possible.

What If Your Husband Gains Full Custody?

What if your husband keeps forcing you to go back to court over and over? What if you run out of money? Or suppose you have done everything you could and the judge rules against you? You wind up with no visitation rights, or limited ones. If you do all you can and still lose custody, it is understandable that you feel devastated. But you can still create a good life. Maybe you can't figure out why you lost your case. But if you do know, try to make changes so you can try again in a year or two. Different circumstances could result in a new court order. Plan for that time. Attend a community college. Train for a new job. Keep meeting with your support team for courage and comfort.

Many women have survived what seemed an intolerable situation. They have learned to live with it. When their children are older, they often understand that their mothers did their best. Even after years of separation they are able to form loving relationships.

Chapter 16

△

Teen Abuse

Some teenage women live with the men who abuse them. Some are married and some have children. If that's your case, most of this book should be helpful. But maybe you're a teenager without children. Perhaps you don't live with your boyfriend. If so, this chapter is especially for you.

Abuse of teenage women by their boyfriends is widespread. Between 25 and 40 percent of teens have been assaulted by dates. About 80 percent of the assaults are pushing, shoving, slapping, and grabbing. But some of the violence is worse, and the worst injuries happen when the abuser is drunk.

Teen men are not the only ones hitting. Teenage women hit their boyfriends, too. But no matter who is causing the abuse, serious damage can be done, especially if a weapon is used. Teen men are usually able to cause more harm than teen women. Most women are not as large or as strong as men, so most men are not afraid of women. While women can be emotionally abusive, they rarely control men.

Many teens are raped by their dates and boyfriends.

Some teen men think it is alright to force women to have sex. They think it is all right if the man has spent money on her, or if she has kissed him. Some teenage women even believe that.

Part of standing up for your rights is knowing that this is *not* all right. It is knowing that forced sex is a form of abuse. Forced sex is rape.

How to Tell If You're Abused

Sometimes it's hard for a teenager to tell whether she's being abused. Teens often play rough and tease each other. This can sometimes turn into physical or emotional abuse. Here are some examples:

You are playfully wrestling with your boyfriend. He twists your arm behind your back. He's hurting you but won't let go until you're crying. Or he throws you into a swimming pool "just in fun." Or he takes your purse and shows people private things in it.

You feel embarrassed, scared, or furious, but you laugh to show you're a good sport. If you don't laugh, your boyfriend says you can't take a joke. You try to make yourself think he's right.

Some teasing is emotional abuse. Maybe your boyfriend makes a habit of "jokes" that embarrass you. He may say insulting things about your body, your friends, or women in general. Maybe he puts down women as "broads" or "chicks." Or maybe he calls attention to your large breasts or thin legs. The "jokes" and insults become a *pattern* that you don't know how to stop.

Perhaps you tell yourself he doesn't know he's hurting your feelings. If that's the case, explain it to him. Be serious; tell him without laughing, flirting, or apologizing. He may say he still doesn't understand. He may say you're too sensitive or have no sense of humor. Tell him you want him to stop whether he understands or not.

If he doesn't stop, it's because he doesn't care how you feel. He may even tease you on purpose to make you feel bad about yourself. Either way, he's wearing down your self-esteem. He's abusing you emotionally.

Teen men practice many other forms of abuse. Some are emotional. Some are physical. Some are a combination of both.

Cars offer some young men a way to show their power. They may speed or drive recklessly to scare their girlfriends. If you feel scared or helpless, insist that your boyfriend stop the car. You have a right to get out whenever you want to.

Your boyfriend may force sex on you. Maybe you've told him you don't want sex. He says that he will find another girlfriend. Or that if you really loved him, you'd let him do what he wants. Or that since you "led him on," he has a right to intercourse. But that's not true. Your body belongs to you.

Maybe you've told your boyfriend to use a condom. You want to make sure you don't get a sexually transmitted infection or AIDS or become pregnant. But he refuses; maybe he tells you that you don't need birth control and that he will handle it.

You know that none of these things is safe. But your boyfriend insists. You're afraid to refuse him. You're afraid he might leave you, or that he will hit you. This is abuse.

Who's Responsible for the Violence?

Usually when a man hits a woman, it's more dangerous than when she hits him. Suppose you punch your boyfriend on the arm or pound his chest. He may be three to ten inches taller than you. Maybe he's also thirty to a hundred pounds heavier. He might not even try to protect himself.

But if you go on hitting him, some day he might become angry. He might hit you with his fist. That's likely to hurt and scare you. So he might keep doing it, to control you. Then he might blame you because after all, you started it.

If you did start it, you should take responsibility for what you did. Hitting is wrong. But that doesn't mean you're responsible for what *he* did. Only he can start or stop his violence. Only you can start or stop yours.

What to Do If You're Hit

If your boyfriend slaps, pushes, or threatens you, you should take it seriously. If he's injured you, it's serious. It means he's willing to use physical force to control you. It could get worse if you don't put a stop to it. You have to make it absolutely clear you won't allow it.

You must do more than complain. Make sure your boyfriend knows that hitting you is *serious*. That it is *wrong*. And that it is *dangerous*. If he knows but hits you anyway, then he doesn't care about you.

He may say that he cares, and that he "couldn't help it." He tells you he won't do it again. He says it's something that "just happened." It was something "out of control."

What if that's really true? Then he can't be sure it won't happen again. So his promises don't mean anything.

He may have hit you "accidentally" or he may have hit you on purpose. Either way, he needs help that you can't give him. He might be helped by a counselor or by a kind of group counseling for men who abuse their partners. If he says he hit you because he was drunk, he also needs help. He needs alcohol-control treatment.

You can insist that he go to counseling or Alcoholics Anonymous. But if you do, you have to be ready to follow through. You have to risk losing him. Suppose you say, "If you don't go, I'll leave you." And suppose he refuses to go? If you stay with him anyway, that tells him you didn't mean it. He can go on hitting you.

Think clearly about what you really are ready to do. Don't make threats you're not sure you'll carry out. It's better to say something you *know* you can do, such as: "I'm not going to see you for a couple of days" or "If you drink when we date, I'll take a bus home."

You can live up to plans like those. And each time you do, you'll feel stronger.

Ending a Relationship

Deciding to break up can be very hard for a teenage woman. It might be especially hard if your relationship was sexual. You may think you can't have another lover for a long, long time. If you do, you're afraid you'll be seen as "loose" or "a slut."

Even if that's not worrying you, you may hesitate. Like many women, you may be afraid that you'll never find another man. It's hard to realize that there are other, better men out there. You've been so wrapped up in your abusive boyfriend, you haven't noticed.

It can help a lot to discuss your problems with an understanding person. As a teenager, you may be afraid to confide in anyone. You worry that a doctor, minister, or teacher might tell your parents. He or she might send your boyfriend away before you've decided what you want. But among people you know, there's probably someone you can talk to safely. It might be a trusted adult or teenage friend. Try talking to your friend now, even if it's painful.

This is the time to talk things over and to think things through. Should you stay in this relationship as a life sentence for a mistake? Many adult battered women were teenagers when they started dating abusive men. Or should you give yourself a second chance at a better life? It's the only life you have. There's time left in it for a lot of good things for you.

Chapter 17

△

Lesbian Abuse

It is hard for almost any woman to admit she's been abused. If you are a lesbian, it might seem as if you are the only one who has experienced abuse. But more and more lesbians have come out of the "second closet." They have spoken out. They are getting help from their communities. If you are a lesbian who's been abused by your partner, this chapter is for you.

Most of *You Can Be Free* is written for women who are abused by men. However, you can substitute "her" where we say "him." Lesbians' situations are significantly different from heterosexuals'. Even so, patterns of abuse are similar.

You will need to modify a few things for your situation. For instance, the information and advice about police and prosecutors may not be right for you. The way police treat lesbians may be very different from the way they treat heterosexuals. Questions about custody differ, too. Your safety plan depends partly on your identity. It also depends on the attitudes and biases of people in the justice system. They vary from one community to another.

How to Identify Abuse

Chapters 1 and 2 help you recognize abuse. Like battering by men, lesbian abuse can be physically dangerous. Maybe your partner has physically or sexually assaulted you. Perhaps the violence has increased or has hurt you more. Such escalations can signal a danger of very serious injuries the next time you are assaulted. A broken jaw or a broken back is a clear sign of danger. Emotional abuse is dangerous, too, and its results may last a long, long time. But it can be hard to identify, and you may not take it seriously. That is why we encourage you to answer the questions in Activity 1 in Chapter 2. Your answers to them will help you identify how emotional abuse has affected you. That is why we focus below on forms of emotional abuse that can be confusing.

The Power of Manipulation

Your partner might have told friends that you are battering her. She might even have persuaded you that is true. If you accuse her of mistreating you, she says, "*You* do that to *me.*" There might be some truth to that. But abuse is about control of another person. It is not one incident. It is a *pattern of abuse of power.*

Abuse can take subtle forms. Pay special attention to the questions in Activity 1 about feeling worn down. Your partner might persuade you she is emotionally or physi-cally fragile. Notice whether she wheedles you into doing things for her. It may not feel as if you're responding to demands. You might give in over and over because the alternative wears you out. The alternative may be anger, rejection, or complaints about her suffering. You wonder why you feel resentful when she is so weak. She says you abuse her and you begin to believe it.

You have energy and strength. You ask yourself, "Why shouldn't I do more than 50 percent of the work?" Besides, you are not "locked in the house" the way "battered wom-en" are. You are just too tired to want to go anywhere. Your partner may be exploiting your strength by using her "weakness." That is one way some people manipulate oth-ers' feelings. Ask yourself what would happen if you did not give in. If that thought fills you with dread, it is prob-ably a sign of abuse. Try refusing to give in. Then evaluate the consequences.

Here's another question that may clarify things. Are you able to live with integrity? You may believe deceit is wrong, yet you lie. You lie to protect her. ("She didn't really hurt me." "She is just under stress.") You lie to save your-self from being abused. ("I didn't spend that much." "I was not out all day.") What would happen if you stopped lying? Would you dread telling the truth?

What If You Both Behave Abusively?

Suppose you have hit your partner or said mean things. You can determine to stop doing those things. But also ask yourself, "What are the consequences of that behavior? Does it enable me to control her?" "Is she afraid of me? Is that the only way I can be safe?" "What about her? When she acts that way, does it help her control me?" "Am I afraid of her? Am I 'walking on eggshells'?"

Suppose you both hit equally often and hard? That means double danger for each of you. Whether your partner wants it or not, you need to get help. Suppose you think you are the one who batters. If you assault or emotionally abuse your partner, start changing now. You cannot change her, but you can change yourself. It will be easier if you separate from her. That will give you a chance to look at what you have done. Find a counselor or group to work on your problem.

If you are being physically abused, your safety is at stake. If you're emotionally or sexually abused, you might feel bewildered. Taking time away from your partner can help you analyze the situation. You'll get to know yourself again. And to like yourself again. You can spend time with friends who value you.

If you believe you are abused, something is seriously wrong. The label may not be so important. But ask yourself whether you are getting what you want from the relationship. This may be the time to consider serious changes. What will happen if you say that to your partner? If the thought of it scares you, you need to talk to someone you can trust.

Ending Isolation

Chapters 11 and 12 suggest ways to overcome your isolation. Your first job is to look out for your own health and safety. If you have children, that will enable you to look after their well-being too. No one should have to do that alone. You will need support.

Isolation may not be only physical. Perhaps you are in touch with friends and family, but you're afraid to tell them the truth. Maybe you're afraid a lesbian friend won't listen to anything about lesbian abuse. She might feel threatened by the idea. Maybe she is also your partner's friend. She won't believe that her friend could abuse you. Think carefully about whom to ask for help. It's important to find people who believe you.

Maybe it has been hard to come out of the closet with your parents or others. It took them a while to accept your lesbian identity. They have begun to like your partner. How can you tell them what she is doing to you? If you think telling would disrupt your family relationship, find someone else to talk to. If you are struggling to decide who, call the National Domestic Violence Hotline at 800/799-SAFE (800/799-7233), or TTY 800/787-3224. Talk over your problem with a domestic violence advocate. You might also get a number from her for a local lesbian or domestic violence hotline.

Meanwhile, try speaking to one friend. Talk about lesbian battering in general. If your friend seems sympathetic, go on to talk about your situation. But if it is too stressful, keep looking for someone you can trust. You need the help of at least one understanding, caring person. It is hard to endure abuse. It is also hard to stop it and to get away from it. Don't go through that alone.

Confidentiality at Counseling and Other Agencies

If you haven't a friend or family member you can trust, look for a counselor. She should be someone who knows about battering and about lesbian lifestyles. If you're "out," you'll likely know which counseling services are available to lesbians. But you might not be sure of their attitudes about domestic violence. Call and ask. Ask whether the program includes help for abused women. Ask about counselors. Do they understand battering as well as lesbian issues? Do they know how police and courts treat battered lesbians?

Even if you are "out," you may still worry that someone will find out about the abuse. Maybe you won't want to risk getting help in your own community. You may not want anyone to know who is battering you. Maybe you don't want anybody to know it's happening at all. Even if the agency has trained counselors who can help, you might be concerned about confidentiality. Ask about the records the agency keeps. Who is allowed to read the files? Where are the files kept? How detailed are they? If you want to read them, how do you get them? Don't accept vague answers.

Ruth was afraid of Robin's violence. But she was also afraid of being known as a lesbian. It was risky for her to be visible. "Robin would call and say, 'Come back or I'm going to tell your job you're a lesbian' or 'I'm going to tell your family.' The job thing didn't matter much, but my family did."

Suppose you're in the closet. You may be afraid to tell anyone about the abuse. Telling might take you out of the closet before you are ready. You need to confide in someone you're sure won't gossip. If you plan to see a counselor or join a group for abused lesbians, will it be safe? Is it a place where people might see you come and go? Will they know you are there because of abuse? Encountering community acquaintances can put you at risk. Keep looking until you find a program in a safe place.

An agency for lesbians may have limited services. Perhaps there's no special program for abused women. But there might be a more general support or therapy group. If it is safe, talk to the leader about discussing abuse in her group. Does she think group members would be accepting? Would she support you no matter what decisions you make? If it is not safe to risk your partner's hearing about it, you may want to go somewhere else.

Some mainstream groups for abused women welcome lesbians. You might feel even safer seeing a counselor who has a private practice. Just be sure she is completely comfortable with a lesbian client and knowledgeable about abuse. A counseling agency for lesbians might recommend someone. You can also call shelters and Safe Homes.

Emergency Services

If the possibility that you might need emergency services has crossed your mind even once, it's best to be prepared. If you're not in a crisis now, this is the best time to gather information.

In an emergency you can find crisis counseling at a hotline for battered women. An advocate there might also give you tips on housing, welfare, and police. In each instance, ask whether what she says applies to lesbians. If she doesn't know, ask her to find out. That can save you from a round of stressful telephone calls. It can also add to the agency's information. That can benefit the next lesbian caller.

Police

Maybe your partner is dangerous. But you're not willing to leave her. That means you may someday need help from police. Your safety plan should include checking on current police treatment of abused lesbians. Ask advocates at your local shelter. If they don't know, ask who does. It is important to be able to call on police for help. But some departments or individual officers know nothing about lesbian abuse. If they are called, they might arrest both parties. Read the general information about police in Chapter 8. But adapt it to your circumstances.

Emergency Housing

In some communities, emergency housing may be limited. In large cities there may be more options. You might feel safest in a Safe Home with a family. Safe Homes are run by agencies that usually have a hotline. So call to find out as much as you can long before you need emergency help.

You might want to go to a shelter for a few days or weeks. Ask questions similar to those we suggested for finding a counselor. Some shelters have lesbian and heterosexual advocates who welcome all women. But staff attitudes can't guarantee how other residents feel. Some battered lesbians in shelters have pretended they were heterosexual. But that can be hard. You are the only one who can decide.

Support from Your Lesbian Community

Being open about abuse can help you—if it is safe. In the long run it might also benefit the whole lesbian community. It's a message that you're not to blame and that you're not ashamed. It can also be a message to your community: "Yes, this is really happening in our own backyard. Isn't it time we did something about it?" Some lesbian communities are already doing exactly that. You can search for them on the Internet or through the national hotline.

Support is out there. Keep searching until you find people who will listen and understand and lend a hand.

Chapter 18

△

Rural Women

"Rootedness in the land is integral to our sense of self. . . . A battered woman [fleeing] the countryside suffers not only the trauma of abuse, but loses an essential component of her rooted identity."
—NCADV Rural Task Force Resource Packet

Why a Special Chapter?

As the quote above indicates, attachment to the land can create a difficult conflict for an abused rural woman. Sociologists now recognize that just as there are ethnic cultures, there is a "rural culture." But "rural culture" doesn't mean just farms. Only about 10 percent of rural residents are full-time farmers. Most work in towns or cities. The few available jobs do not pay well. So life in rural communities can be hard for many residents.

Some studies find that religion is more important to rural people than to urban people. Rural people are more likely to know each other's business. Still, rural Appalachia is very different from rural upstate New York or rural Alaska. Native Americans on a reservation are different from Mexican fruit pickers. Living on a farm is not much like staying in an abandoned trailer. Or in a small house half a mile from the one church, tavern, and general store in the area. Even within each of those situations, people have different values.

Growing up in the countryside may encourage similar perspectives. Researchers say rural people are suspicious of outsiders. They distrust government. Everyone knows the neighbors' business. Some think those are negative traits. The flip side is that people tend to be self-reliant. Most Americans value that trait. Knowing about each other can also mean they look out for each other.

Rural people tend to have larger extended families. They can be a source of support. But close traditional families can cause problems, too. Researchers say rural people tend to hold similar values about family. Wives should stay at home and obey their husbands. Husbands go out to work. Men and women value family relationships more than city folks. This doesn't mean all rural people think alike. These are tendencies. City people value family, too. But other things are sometimes as important.

You might have good reasons for not wanting to leave your husband. You might be afraid that will mean giving up your community. Maybe you live in a farmhouse that has been in your family for generations. Maybe you simply love the landscape. Your family and friends are there. These pulls are easy to understand.

People picture rural life as peaceful. But the amount of family violence is about the same in cities, suburbs, and rural areas. That includes wife battering and child abuse. In some rural families, life is not so tranquil, after all.

Domestic abuse can be more dangerous in rural areas. There are more hunters and more readily available guns. In the countryside the sound of a gunshot might go unnoticed. Yet guns are usually more dangerous than fists. An abuser who owns a gun might use it as a threat. Sociologist Neil Websdale quotes a woman in rural Kentucky:

> "He'd shoot somethin'. He'd say, 'That could be your head, you know.'"

But there is rural and there is rural. Life in the hills of Kentucky is very different from that in an area full of migrant workers. Many such families do not speak English. They rarely contact English speakers. They may not know U.S. laws. Those without legal documents may fear contact with police.

In many kinds of rural areas police and sheriffs do not take abuse seriously. It can be frightening to report battering. The only officer might be your husband's brother. A rural sheriff in Virginia once said, "A man comes home after a few drinks, slaps his wife—do you call that abuse?" Many grim examples show how rural women are mistreated by the law. But things are slowly changing. The U.S. government has recognized the unfairness of scarce services in many rural areas.

Maybe you are a Native American who lives on a rural reservation. You cope with the same problems as other rural women. But you face additional challenges. Native tribes have a right to make their own laws. The mix of U.S. and tribal laws is confusing. You might even say it is "crazy-making." Some Native American women say they are neglected by state programs. In 1993 in one area of 20,000 Native women, only one rape victim received services.

But many Native American women are organizing to struggle against intimate violence. In many Indian tribes and communities men and women are working together to stop violence. The federal government has funded many rural Indian projects. (You can find much information on the Internet. See our Resources section.)

Not only Native Americans suffer from neglect in rural areas. Women who are emotionally and physically abused need many services. Yet few are available. Rarely are there enough police or sheriffs. The prosecutor might work only half time. If you leave your partner, it may be hard to stay in the community. It may be impossible to find a job to support several kids. Government agencies provide little money for rural schools. Vocational training and higher education are scarce. Health-care workers are in short supply. Untreated illness and dental problems lead to exhaustion. That makes it harder to struggle against abuse. Even insurance companies decline to operate in rural areas. Public transportation is rarely available.

Still, a medical clinic is likely to be your best source of help. Federal funds now support special rural abused women's programs. Some include an advocate who works in a clinic. If your community has those services, you can see a doctor without your neighbor knowing why you're there. So if there is a clinic in your nearest town, try to get the doctor to help.

But many doctors will not ask you about an injury. You may have to ask directly for help. Describe the abuse precisely. Use blunt words such as, "He hit me." A doctor or nurse can call an advocate for you. She might even testify in court. If you don't feel safe confiding in your doctor, try to go to a clinic in a nearby community. It might be easier to talk about the abuse to someone you don't know.

Making a Safety Plan

Whether you want to leave or stay, being safe may be a major challenge. You might think there is no safety in a city. Yet a reliable safety plan may be even harder to carry out in a rural area. Consider your fears and the pros and cons of leaving home. Include the things you would miss if you left. Be sure to list city resources that can make life easier. Better schools. Nearby clinics. Child care. Easy transportation. A community college. Most of all a safe shelter.

Consider a Permanent Move

The idea of leaving home permanently may seem extreme and scary. But if you carefully consider the possibility, you will feel more confident. You will know you made the best decision possible. Consider each thing you hate to leave at home. Can you find it somewhere else? Then ask what scares you about moving to a new community. Are you thinking about a really big city? You might consider moving to another rural town where you will be safer. It could have many of the things you love about your hometown. You could move to a city that is not so big it makes you nervous. Once you know what scares you, then you can find out more about it. You might even discover something you will like.

Try to think of what you could gain in the new place. In a city, a loss might also be a gain. For instance, "many strangers." The positive is that police and judge "strang-

Activity 14   *Leaving and Staying— A Balancing Act*

	Leaving Rural Home for a City		Staying Home	
	Good	*Bad*	*Good*	*Bad*
1.	Being safe	Leaving my animals	I'm on the land	Risking my life
2.	More jobs	Many strangers	It's what I know	Living with fear
3.	_____	_____	_____	_____
4.	_____	_____	_____	_____
5.	_____	_____	_____	_____
6.	_____	_____	_____	_____

ers" won't know your husband's family. The negative is that strangers pay little attention to you. But you might be much safer where no one notices you. No one can tell the abuser where you are. Try hard to list the positive and negative aspects of both staying in the country and leaving for a city. Then consider a town that offers transportation, good jobs, or a community college. Ask the same questions about it.

Put a question mark beside the items you think you

would like. Put a check mark by ones you're afraid you wouldn't like. See how the two sides measure up. How many question marks are there? Maybe some things are so important they outweigh everything else. Your safety might be one. Are you willing to leave everything you love to ensure your safety? Are you willing to risk serious injury or even death rather than leave your family and home? Call an advocate. Ask her to listen to you talk about those questions. She can tell you about cities and towns nearby.

Help from an Advocate

To find an advocate, call a hotline or shelter. You can call the toll-free national line: 800/799-SAFE (800/799-7233) or TTY 800/787-3224. You can talk over your questions with an advocate on the phone. But you can also ask her for the number of a hotline near you.

An advocate helps an abused woman evaluate her risks. If you haven't read Chapter 1, you may want to do that before you call. An advocate will respect your attachment to a rural way of life. She will know of safe places for you to meet her at, such as a library, grocery store, or police station. She will know the places that are *generally* safe. You will know the places that are safe *for you*. You will avoid any place the abuser is likely to pass by. You will be careful not to let a neighbor see you talking to a stranger. If the advocate is well known because of the work she does, you will want to be especially careful that no one sees you with her.

Together you and the advocate can make the best choice for a safe and private meeting place. But you may have to be near a bus or taxi or have access to a car. Often those are not options. Maybe you can get a friend to drive you to a meeting place. But talking on the phone could be a better choice. Of course, that assumes you have a phone. Or that the abuser does not take it when he leaves. That is why meeting or telephoning from a clinic may be your best bet.

An advocate on the national hot line can tell you whether there is a nearby shelter or Safe Home. She won't tell anyone about your call. But if you worry that the local person who answers will be someone you know, ask for the number of a shelter fifty or one hundred miles away.

Someone who knows your own community can help you complete your plan. But your second choice might be someone who understands your way of life. That could be a member of your tribe, ethnic group, race, or your rural culture, whether in your state or across the country.

Help from a Shelter or Safe Home

Maybe you only want to get away for a day or two. You just want to talk to someone knowledgeable about abuse and rural life. You need help in deciding what to do. First you will have to find a way to ask someone to help.

In a desperate moment, you might have to walk or run a long way to escape an abuser. But that could also be dangerous. It may even be impossible, especially if you have children or if you are physically unstable or injured. So try to plan ahead of time what to do in the worst situation. Decide where you will go and how you will get there. A review of Chapters 1 and 7 and the safety plan at the beginning of the book can help. Know who can help you, but be careful whom you confide in. The wrong person could also make it harder to get away.

Suppose you are always with the person who abuses you. You might not have access to a private phone. But try to find one person who understands your situation. Show her your bruises if you have them. Ask for help. Try to find a reason to be at her house. Maybe you will have to go there with your husband. Before you go, try to talk to her privately. Ask her to put a wireless or cell phone in the bathroom. A few minutes after you get to her house, excuse yourself. Go to the bathroom and call the hotline. Be ready with your questions, and keep the conversation short. Try to keep the abuser from knowing what you are doing. That will help you get another chance. Then call again. Ask more questions.

It may take several calls to get what you need. This is difficult, but each woman does what she can, in the way she can.

Although rural professionals sometimes lack adequate training, Neil Websdale interviewed a number of rural women who were helped by them.

> *"If it wasn't for the social worker at Social Services*
> *. . . I don't know how I would have made it. . . ."*

> *"Thank God the social worker spoke up for me. . . ."*

Like those rural women, with a little help you too can make new decisions and create a safer life.

Chapter 19

△

Immigrant Women: Challenges and Solutions

"I can't tell anyone outside my community; they'll think we're terrible people."

"I tried to tell my mother but she said I've shamed the family."

"If I call the police, they'll arrest my husband and deport him."

"I can't speak English, can't drive, and don't have a paid job. So how could I make it on my own?"

Does this sound like you? If so, you are not alone. It is frightening to be abused, especially if you are an immigrant. It might feel as if everywhere you turn you find more problems. But in the United States physical and sexual abuse are against the law. That means you can find people to help you keep yourself and your children safe.

An abusive man can use your fears to intimidate you.

Maybe you don't know much about U.S. culture. You might not speak English. Or you depend on your husband for your immigration status. An abusive man will use all of that to control you. Has he said he will apply for your green card but then not done it? Does he make fun of your accent? This is a good time to do Activity 1 in Chapter 2. Other chapters give information for any woman who is abused. But this chapter is especially for abused *immigrant* women.

Assessing a Safety Plan for Staying or Leaving

Look at the safety plan at the beginning of the book. It gives you ideas about what *might* increase your safety. But read Chapter 1 too. It tells you how to adapt safety plans for your own situation. What is safe for a citizen may not be for a refugee. Once you name your risks, you may be able to reduce their danger.

Even if you stay with your abusive partner, you might have to leave in an emergency. If you do, you will have to make quick decisions. You will need certain papers and supplies. If you plan, you will have gathered the things you need. You will have put them where you can easily get them. You will know where to go to be safer and how to get there fast.

Documents to Keep in a Safe Place

If you have to leave in an emergency, you may have to stay away longer than you would like. While you are gone your husband may destroy papers needed for court or that show your immigration status. You will need to put copies of these important papers in a safe place:

- Your immigration papers
- Your husband's immigration papers
- Your and his drivers' licenses
- Proof of marriage or similar relationship (wedding certificate; wedding photos; love letters; envelopes, bills, or rent receipts addressed to both you and your husband)
- Medical records
- Records of police reports
- Children's school records, birth certificates, medical records

Begin to collect the items you can as soon as safely possible. Keep medicines, prescriptions, and eyeglasses in a safe place too.

Maybe you are sure you will never leave or divorce your husband. Keep your documents safe anyway. An abusive person is likely to destroy or hide important documents. They should be where you can easily get them. You may want them even if you are gone for only a few weeks. But act carefully. Otherwise you could be in more danger instead of less.

Copy the papers and be sure to return the originals to their places. If your husband knows what you've done, he might punish you. Leave the copies with someone you trust. Knowing you can get them when you want can increase your confidence. That will help you make the best choice. Each step of your plan—if you follow it carefully—brings you closer to safety. Keep reminding yourself of that.

Advocates and Shelters for Abused Immigrant Women

"Advocate" means a worker in a domestic abuse shelter or hotline. She has special training in domestic violence. Local advocates can give you valuable information. You can also telephone 800/799-SAFE (800/799-7233) or TTY 800/787-3224. Those are national numbers. But advocates there can find you information about help in your own community. You might have questions about your immigration status. You can ask an advocate how to safely get the information you need. *It is not a good idea to go to the U.S. immigration office until you have reliable information.* (INS is the old term for Immigration and Naturalization Service. It changed its name to the U.S. Citizen and

Immigration Service or USCIS. Everyone will know what you mean if you say "CIS" or "INS.") First, ask an advocate to help you find an attorney. Find out what you can expect, given your immigration status. It is important to consult an attorney who understands immigration law *and* domestic violence.

Try to find an agency where advocates understand your language and culture. Look for one that specializes in helping immigrants who have experienced domestic violence. Advocates in such agencies will usually know how your local police and courts treat abused women. They will also know how immigrants are treated. That is especially necessary if you live in a town near a national border. They can tell you about programs for men who batter. They know how to search for financial aid and housing. They can find experts to advise you about your immigration status.

They can give you expert advice on how to make a safety plan. They will not tell you what to do. They know there are reasons to stay and reasons to leave an abusive partner. They can tell you what to expect if you call the police. Maybe you want to separate. It is hard to talk about it in English. But advocates can help you find people who understand. They can find a safe place for you to stay for a few days or longer. They can help you escape and reorganize your life safely. It is important to learn as much as you can about your options. They can help you change your life.

Asha, an abused Somali woman, could not speak English. But an advocate in an agency serving abused immigrant women helped her enroll in an English class. She showed Asha how to get a court order to keep her husband away and how to enroll in a professional child-care course. Now she has a job and she and her children are safer.

Maybe you worry about going to a shelter. You might wonder whether you will be able to follow your religious or cultural dietary customs. But almost any shelter can see that you have vegetarian meals or have your food served on paper plates. Those two arrangements may take care of most of your needs. If not, ask for what you want or need.

Divorce or Separation: Immigration Status

You might want to know whether you can leave your husband permanently and stay in the United States. That depends partly on what kind of resident status you have. It could also depend on his status. But immigration laws have changed. They have opened new doors to applying for legal residency. You may not have to depend on your spouse's status anymore. The law is very complicated, so you need expert help. *See an immigration lawyer who specializes in abuse.*

The application process for citizenship may take a very long time. Even getting a green card or work permit can take years. You need to check with an immigration expert to find out what status you can apply for. Then you submit your papers and you might be asked to fill out more paperwork. Immigration services must officially inform you of their decision. If necessary, a legal advocate can help you find an expert in another town to consult by phone.

> *For Anju, a South Asian woman, it was only safe to phone an advocate when her husband was out. After a few calls, the advocate found her an immigration attorney knowledgeable about domestic abuse. It took a long time to gather all her documents, plus two more years of waiting. But now she has a green card. For Anju, the waiting was hard but worthwhile. If your case takes a long time to settle, try to be patient. Just keep checking. Changes might make you eligible.*

To Call the Police or Not

For general information about police and prosecutors, read Chapter 8, "Getting Help from Professionals." It offers ideas for any abused woman and describes what might happen if you call the police. But an immigrant will have other concerns. What might you gain and lose if your husband is sent out of the country? Fear of being deported can keep you from acting to protect yourself.

Think now about what you will do if your life is in danger. Before you need it, ask an English speaker to prepare a card for you that says, "I do not speak English. I speak ____." Keep the card with you all the time. Remember you have a legal right to remain silent.

Maybe you want to learn English, but your husband forbids it. It could be risky to attend a class secretly. You may be able to enlist your children's help. Learn a few important phrases, such as "Help!" Learn how to say "My name is ____. I live at ____. I am in danger. I speak ____." If you ever need to call police, that may save your life.

Maybe you don't have a phone. Try to find a neighbor or friend who will let you use hers in an emergency. If you are attacked or threatened, dial 911—if it is safe. Explain what has been done to you. The 911 operator can see what address the call came from. So you don't have to worry about speaking English well. But if you use a cell phone, you will have to tell the 911 operator exactly where you are. The 911 dispatcher will probably send an officer and a medical team. If you need to go to a hospital, they will take you there.

When the police arrive, show them any signs of injury even if it seems embarrassing. Ask for a translator. Or hand the officer the card mentioned above. It is *not* a good idea to rely on your children for translations. Friends may want to help. But you need a professional translator. Be sure it is someone who is not part of immigration services. American law states that you have a right to a translator.

If you want the police to take action, do not tell them everything is fine. Once they are gone, your husband might become even more violent. He might punish you for calling. Or maybe the police will arrest him. Then they might suggest you can stay home in safety. But there is no way to tell how long he will stay in jail. You need time away from him to decide what to do next. You might want to bring up several questions with an advocate. Is your husband likely to be deported? Is that what you want? Those questions are complicated. It can take time to gather information about them, and then to decide what you want. Ask the police to take you to a shelter. Or to help you find transportation to another safe place for the night.

Awareness Shifts; Attitudes Change

Members of your community may have learned that battering is a crime. Customs vary even within traditional cultures. You may be pretty sure you know what your community thinks about controlling husbands. But is that what everyone believes? What about marital separations? In conversations, watch for openings. Then—if it's safe—raise questions about marital violence or divorce. Listen carefully to the responses. You don't have to say what you think about it. Some opinions might surprise you. Keep listening. Find someone who understands the problem in the same way you do. That person may help you keep yourself and your children safer.

After living in the United States for years, many immigrants change. So do other people, including the police. Maybe in the past your appeals to your community or police were rejected.

> *Tukata, a Laotian woman, was abused by her husband. She was told, "That's just the way it is." But five years later neighbors helped her and police took her more seriously. Together, they probably saved Tukata's life. Circumstances change. People change. With help from other people, you can change too, if that is what you want.*

Know Your Rights

If any governmental official (police officer, FBI agent, or Immigration official) wishes to engage you in conversation, all persons—citizens and noncitizens—have the constitutional right to remain silent and request a lawyer. You should know that *anything* you say to a police officer can be used against you. Thus, if a police officer or other governmental official wishes to ask you questions about a suspected crime, you have the right to tell the officer: "I wish to remain silent; I want to speak to a lawyer." You do not have to say anything else.

If the police, FBI, or Immigration come to your home, you have the right to refuse them entry, unless they produce a warrant from a judge. If the officials do not have a search warrant, you do not have to let them into your home. You have the right to say "I do not want to talk to you until I have spoken to a lawyer." If you give them permission to enter, they may enter legally. If you throw the door open and wave them in, you are probably giving permission. You should say politely that you do not want to speak to them, that they do not have permission to enter your home, and that if they leave a number, your lawyer will call them.

Your skin color, accent, or the language you speak are not lawful reasons for an immigration agent or other officer to question, detain, threaten, or arrest you. Your color or the language you speak do not legally justify a presumption that you are not a U.S. citizen. You do not have to speak to an immigration agent. However, if you answer their questions, including questions about where you were born, that may give them a "reasonable suspicion" that you are not a citizen.

You have the right to speak to an attorney before answering any questions or signing any documents. You should *never* sign documents without first speaking to an immigration attorney. If an immigration agent or any other officer approaches you, the safest thing to do is to say that you don't want to talk, ask to speak with your lawyer, and remain silent. It is a crime to lie to a federal official or other law enforcement officer. It is safer to say that you don't want to talk, and then remain silent until you contact a lawyer.

If you are accused of something that makes you deportable, you will have the right to a hearing with an immigration judge and the right to have an attorney represent you at that hearing and in any interview with Immigration (there are no government-paid lawyers, as there are in criminal proceedings, however). Do not give up this right. Insist on a hearing, especially if you are detained.

Unless you have already gone through a whole proceeding and already have a final, unappealed deportation order, immigration cannot just grab you and take you to the plane and deport you. You do get a day in court. Don't sign anything that gives it up.

Adapted with permission from the Northwest Immigration Rights Project

Chapter 20

△

Women with Disabilities

Cowritten by Cathy Hoog

"Had I not been blind," Susan said, "he would have chosen another vehicle by which to intimidate me. My disability was just the most convenient means available. It afforded him a myriad of ways to control and strike fear into me, to make me really begin to believe I was crazy. . . ."

Approximately 250 million women in the world have a disability. Some physical conditions are obvious. But many are largely invisible. Among those are mental illness, learning problems, drug addiction, seizure disorders, and diabetes. Many other illnesses are increasing. Abusers use anything available to control another person. In this chapter we offer ways to create a safety plan especially for your situation. You may be abused by your husband or a caretaker. Maybe your husband *is* your caretaker. If so, it is probably painful and frightening to face the truth. But you can figure out what you want and what you're willing to do to get it. You have survived so far by using your strength.

Maybe your disability resulted from an assault by your partner. You might have epileptic seizures from a kick in the head. Maybe you are paralyzed from a blow. You might know the abuser caused the disability on purpose. Focusing on that can make you angry or emotionally frozen. It can cloud your thinking. That is understandable but it doesn't have to stay that way.

> *When Wendy's boyfriend threatened her, she tried to escape. But he shot her and now, at twenty-eight, she is a paraplegic. In high school she was a track and field athlete. She knows that looking back on those days in bitterness will not help her heal. Instead, she focuses on coping with her fears, working at physical therapy, and learning to do things for herself. She refuses to squander precious energy on hatred. "If I hate him," Wendy says, "he will always be on my mind. . . ."*

When the Abuser Plays on Your Fears

"He said he would take my wheelchair away."

"He said he would hurt my kids."

Abusers often know what threats are most frightening. Many threats are more hurtful than physical assaults.

Maybe he tells you that you can't survive without him. Then you are scared of being abandoned. It may be true that your life would be hard without his—or her—caretaking. But it is hard now too. Even if you do need assistance, there may be other places to find it.

What makes it difficult to leave the abuser may also make it risky to stay. The most serious physical harm may be from a physical assault. But disabling your medical equipment can harm you as much as a sock with a fist. The wrong dose of medicine can hurt you as seriously as an attack. But you can find ways to prevent harm and to enhance your safety.

> *Jenny's live-in boyfriend, Tom, had hit her several times, and finally she threatened to call the police. Tom said he would tell them she "had mental problems." He knew Jenny's therapist prescribed medicine to stabilize her emotions. When an officer responded to Jenny's call, Tom said she hallucinated and had probably hit herself. But Jenny, forewarned, had asked her therapist for a statement saying she was stable. She showed it to the officer, who believed her and not Tom. Following her safety plan enabled Jenny to outwit Tom.*

▲ △ ▲

External and Internal Barriers

An abuser tries to make you feel unsure of yourself. That is not hard when society's barriers have some of the same effects. Lack of wheelchair ramps and tactile signs in buildings can prevent you from doing all you are able to do. In spite of barriers, most people with disabilities manage well. You probably have invented a trick or two to deal with everyday glitches. Keep looking for, and thinking of, creative options. Try different ways to do things. If they are hard, practice them. If they don't work, try something else. Now and then check with your doctor or disabilities advocate. A new invention could make your life easier. And safer.

An abuser will probably try to stop you from getting around by yourself. He might act as if he is doing it to be kind. If you are no longer sure what you are able to do, this is a good time to find out. Try not to get bogged down by negative thoughts. Focus on what you *can* do, or *can learn* to do. You may have already overcome some of the abuser's barriers. Gaining control over one area of life can lead to another. And then another.

Analyzing Patterns of Abuse

Analyzing a pattern of emotional abuse can give you ideas about how to minimize the danger. Look at Activity 1 in

Chapter 2. Pay special attention to the items that relate specifically to women with disabilities. Think about your answers to sections A, E, and F. They may suggest you're becoming isolated. The abuser might say he has taken over your care "for your own good." Below, analyze the difference between caretaking and taking control. Fill in your situation.

Activity 15 *Taking Care and Taking Control: What's the Difference?*

Takes Care of Me	Result	What I Want
1. Decides what meds I need	Overdoses me so I feel woozy	To handle meds myself
2. Discusses my treatment with the doctor	He has the info I need	Make decisions myself
3. He is my payee	He has my money	I want a different payee
4. Reads my mail	I have no privacy	A CCTV to enlarge print
5. _____ _____	_____ _____	_____ _____
6. _____ _____	_____ _____	_____ _____
7. _____ _____	_____ _____	_____ _____

Suppose your partner really is trying to do you a favor. You still have a right to tell him what kind of help you want. *If it is safe,* tell him what you want him to do. Let him know what you want to handle yourself. You might want to ask him not to help unless you ask. Setting limits might make him angry. So invite a friend to be with you. If you're afraid to do that, ask yourself what you fear. If it isn't safe to say what you want, you might be in serious danger. If so, it could be time to modify your safety plan. It might even be time to make a plan to leave.

Safety Plans

Each person faces different obstacles from an abuser. Making a safety plan means you pay close attention to every part of your environment. Be sure you overlook nothing. List supportive people. Secure your medicine. Evaluate your strengths. Think of ways to protect your necessary equipment from the abuser's interference. Set aside plenty of time to think of all possible dangers. Think of ways you might prevent them. You may need the help of an advocate to do all that. To find out what advocacy services are available, call the National Domestic Violence Hotline at 800/799-SAFE (800/799-7233) or TTY 800/787-3224.

Building a Support Team

If you can't tell anyone what the abuser is doing, you can't get help. The abuser knows that. If his voice is the only one you hear, he can keep you away from people who can help you. Pretty soon you might believe you deserve his treatment. You may feel alone. But you are not. You just have to find the right supportive people. The more people you can trust who know the truth, the safer you are.

Advocates

A domestic violence advocate can help you think of new ways to protect yourself. A disabilities advocate can build on what she has learned from other women with disabilities. Maybe you want to leave the abuser. If so, an advocate can help you gather information about living on your own. If you want to stay with the abuser, the advocate can help you evaluate the danger and make a safety plan.

Ideally, advocates understand domestic violence *and* disabilities. But you may not find all that expertise in one person. You might have to explain your disability to a domestic violence advocate. You will have to tell her how it affects your life. Then, maybe you'll educate a disabilities advocate about domestic abuse. Let both advocates know you are creating a support team. Encourage them to work together. Ask them to be on your team. You will need others on your team, too. Include friends, relatives—anyone you can trust. Collectively, they might have all the skills you need. You can all pool ideas about safety plans. They can help you evaluate the methods you tried in the past to increase your safety.

Most women who are abused need support from others. Asking people for help is an important part of your safety plan. If it seems safe, tell your rabbi or minister about the abuse. Talk to your doctor, nurse, or rehab counselor. First sound out the person by asking general questions. Find out their attitudes about abuse. Ask how they feel about your living independently. Ask about the possibility of finding a different caretaker. Keep searching until you find someone who listens. Then ask for what you want. You might be surprised at how much help is available.

This is your opportunity to become the best expert on your safety. You know what triggers feelings of insecurity, anger, or confusion. Those reactions make it hard to be your best self. They make it hard to make decisions. Certain phrases commonly used by the abuser might make you anxious when used by someone else. You can let your team know what the triggers are. Together you can come up with the best plan to face them. The information you give the others is essential for them to be able to help you.

Physical Safety Plan

The solutions to problems are as varied as the women. That's why you need to fit your safety plan to your exact needs. You can take dozens of actions to increase your safety and you are the best judge of what to try. If you feel too afraid, try to think of ways to protect yourself from the danger. Then you can consider it again. Here are a few ideas to get you started. You can add to them, depending on your disability and situation. Whether you live with the abusive person or leave, try to get a cell phone and keep it in a secret place. Turn off the ringer. Try to keep the phone with you at all times. Program 911 and other safety numbers into the speed dial of the phone. Erase any numbers you call. Do the same with a TTY.

Leaving in an Emergency: You Can Plan for It

One day you might find yourself in extreme danger. You have no choice but to get to a safe place. It might be for only a day or two. With the help of an advocate, think of all the things you might need. When you're home, you might take many of them for granted. But when you're away, you realize how important they are. Some will be necessary for your safety. If you haven't read Chapter 1, you might want to do that first. Check out the safety plan at the front of the book. Then follow the suggestions in it and in Chapter 7. You will find lists of things you'll need if you have to leave home fast. A major part of your safety plan is to prepare for the worst case. So collect ahead of time the things you will need. Then put them in a safe place. Here are additional items to consider: Medicine, medical information, medic alert systems. Phone numbers of emergency medical support personnel. Social Security award letter/payee information or other benefit information. Supplies for service animals. Spare batteries. Backup assistive devices. Information on how to get replacements for the device if it is damaged. Instructions for technical equipment.

Add any items that are important to your safety or comfort. If you have kids, add any special things they treasure. Have a plan for calling 911 from home or a shelter. Memorize or write the numbers in a secret place. Add critical telephone numbers.

If There Is Time to Prepare to Leave Permanently

If there is a possibility you will leave for good, add telephone numbers for other people who can help you. They might have information on accessible housing or reliable caretakers. You may have to wait a long time for accessible permanent housing. So get started as soon as you can. If possible, alert caseworkers and support staff to your plan ahead of time. Maybe you and the abuser have had the same caseworker. Request to change to a different person. Before you leave, try to open a savings account. Have your benefit checks directly deposited into that account. Find out if you have any new benefits coming. Consider applying for transportation services. Learn your rights. These are all tasks an advocate can help you with.

Living on Your Own

Suppose you leave the abuser. This is a time you could be in the most danger. The abuser may try to find you. He may stalk you. Follow whichever safety measures you used earlier if they still fit your situation. Modify the ones that no longer fit. Include practicing a route of escape. Consider installing an alarm button, intercom, or phone system. Put spy holes in your doors, placed at the correct height for you.

Susan, quoted at the beginning of this chapter, was lucky to have good friends. She was smart to listen to them. They helped her recognize the problem and then they helped her get away safely. Your friends and professional advocates can also help you increase your safety.

Chapter 21

△

Women Who Are Deaf

Cowritten by Cathy Hoog

As a Deaf woman you are probably used to doing things differently from hearing people. The way abuse is carried out will be different too. If you are Deaf, or Deaf-Blind, you have developed visual or tactile ways to communicate. They include how you get information about what is happening around you.

An abuser will try to control you by isolating you. If you are Deaf, he will try to interfere with your communication. He might try to cut you off from emergency services or from support systems that help abused women. The tactic he chooses may depend on whether he is hearing or Deaf.

If the Abuser Is Hearing

An abuser is likely to use any tactic available. He will look for things to do that might upset you. He might grow a moustache to cover his mouth so you can't read his lips. If he interprets for you, he might twist your words or lie about what other people are saying. If he keeps you away from your Deaf friends, they won't be available to tell you the truth. Isolation from your Deaf community can make it hard to get ideas about how other abused Deaf women have kept safe.

Try to make friends. Maybe it isn't safe to approach your husband's hearing friends. Maybe you live in a small town where there is no Deaf community. Possibly you don't know whether there is one or not. If the abuser knows, he may keep you from it. But modern technology is helping Deaf people find each other, sometimes on the Internet. You can ask a friend to let you use her computer, or use one at the library. Be sure it is someplace the abuser can't control. See the technology tips at the end of this chapter.

The abuser may forbid your kids to learn ASL. He might tell them they can't get along without the help of hearing people. He might say that's because Deaf people are inferior to hearing people. If you haven't answered the questions about emotional abuse in Activity 1 in Chapter 2, you might do that now. Your answers will show you what tactics your partner uses and how they affect you. Then you can begin to change the situation. Do all you can to stay connected to your community. They can be your best supporters and help you find services to fit your needs.

If the Abuser Is Deaf

If the abuser is Deaf or a member of the Deaf community, he may try to separate you from your friends or make you embarrassed to talk to them. He might be a teacher, interpreter, or a leader with power in the Deaf community. If he is a Deaf leader, he may think he can turn others against you. But usually people notice when abusers try to make excuses for their behavior. If he is an interpreter, you have a right to ask for a different one. You also have the right to an interpreter who is not his friend. Sometimes waiting for an interpreter you can trust is safer than accepting one you can't trust.

> *Roselle worried because her abusive ex-husband showed up at all the Deaf community events she attended. He made threats and followed her home. She got a protection order and showed it to the director of the organization. He agreed not to allow the abuser in the building while Roselle was there, so she was safer.*

Know Your Rights

Below is a partial list of your rights. If the abuser is not abiding by them, that can signal that his behavior is abusive. You have a right to:

1. Choose the kind of sign language or communication method you want
2. Use your preferred method in public or in private places
3. Ask for help from advocates, police, and others in hearing communities
4. Ask for a change of caseworker or therapist
5. Have an interpreter who is qualified and neutral
6. Control your use of your TTY, telebraille, or other devices
7. Decide when to see friends in the Deaf and hearing communities
8. Obtain public and private services. Ask your advocate about the Americans with Disabilities Act (ADA) guidelines.

Carol, a Deaf woman, was in serious danger from a violent husband. She had good support from the Deaf community in her hometown. But, to isolate her, her husband moved her to another town. When her husband kept her from using sign language with her baby, Carol walked out. She went to a hospital and was taken to a shelter, where a Deaf advocate helped her find ways to be safer and to get back to her hometown support system.

Leaving and Staying

It is not easy to make a decision to stay or to leave a relationship. Maybe your biggest worry is losing contact with your Deaf community. That is an important consideration. Activity 1 in Chapter 2 and Activities 3 and 4 in Chapter 7 can help you weigh its significance against other fears and hopes. Then you can make a decision that is right for you. Deaf women face some challenges that are different from those of other women. Accurate information about your choices will enable you to confront them. Talking to the right advocate can help you do that.

Who in Your Community Can You Trust?

Few women can find safety from an abuser without help from a friend, a family member, or an advocate for abused women. Maybe you have kept the abuse a secret from your family or even your best friend. You might be afraid the news will travel through the Deaf community. You could be in danger if the abuser found out you were breaking the secret about his abuse. Yet if no one knows what is being done to you, that can increase your danger too. So if you decide to confide in someone, it is important to choose carefully.

Think about the people you trust. How do you know whether it is safe to tell others? Where should you start?

What problems do you expect? How much is safe to tell? These are hard questions. An advocate can help you decide where to begin.

Try to find someone who has learned about safety and abuse. Then let her know what has been happening. Explain why you were afraid to tell her what was going on. Let her know how important it is to keep the information to herself. Tell her you are confiding in her because you trust her. Then you can work together to take the next step of letting others know. Maybe she can gather information to help you decide when that is safe. She might help you connect with the services you choose.

As we saw earlier in this chapter, Roselle's Deaf community leader was understanding. That kind of support may not be possible yet in your own community. But maybe you can help create it. More Deaf people are becoming aware of the problem of battering. When everyone seems to know each other, it can be frightening to tell anyone. But in the long term there will be advantages. The more Deaf people talk about the problem, the stronger everyone will become. And the stronger the community, the more able it is to confront abusers.

▲ △ ▲

Advocates Help with Safety Plans

Lots of Deaf women try to find an advocate who understands domestic violence and deafness and Deaf culture. You can call the National Domestic Violence Hotline at 800/787-3224. This TTY hotline is answered nine-to-five by Abused Deaf Women's Advocacy Services' advocates. They will know where to find Deaf advocates and what services are available near you. They will know if a shelter has a TTY or if the advocates understand ASL, or use qualified interpreters. No matter where you live, they can find the closest advocate to fit your needs. After you make any phone calls the abuser might track, be sure to clear the text from your TTY, pager, or computer. If you keep the printouts of risky TTY tapes, make sure they are in a safe place. See the Technology Tips at the end of the chapter.

You may be afraid that an advocate will tell you to leave your partner. But she will know that you need to decide that for yourself. She can help you make a safety plan in case at some time you have to or want to get away. She has a lot of general information gained from talking to other women. You are the one who has specific information about your personal situation. The safety plan can be made as a partnership between you and the advocate. Advocates for Deaf women and advocates for abused women keep strict confidentiality.

Emergency Safety Plan to Leave

You might not want to think about leaving. But "safety first" means making just-in-case plans for things that *could* go wrong. After all, people who have never been sick buy health insurance, just in case. It is good to have a safety plan, even if you never have to use it. An advocate will help you look at what you already do to increase your safety. She will help you evaluate the risk of continuing those actions and of trying new tactics.

First, gather information from an advocate about what help is available in your area. If you have access to the Internet, check out the websites for agencies for Deaf people. Some of them list local services. If you contact them, don't hesitate to ask questions. See the safety plan at the beginning of the book. Gather together everything you might need if you leave home in a hurry. Copy documents you might need, and put everything in a safe place. If you do leave, try to take your TTY if you have one and the cord and batteries. Take extra batteries for your text pager or any other device you use. Be sure you have telephone numbers of interpreters or others who can help you be safe.

Make sure your children know what to do in an emergency. You won't be able to carefully watch an angry abuser at the same time you give directions to your child.

So plan a simple fast signal to your children. They should know where to go and what to do when they hear a click of your fingers, or a certain word.

When Hannah's husband threatened her with a knife, she dialed 911 from the TTY in her bedroom. An officer came, but with her husband watching, Hannah was afraid to say what he had done. Through the interpreter she explained her fears. Then the officer made her husband turn his back so he couldn't see Hannah signing. Speaking up for her rights increased Hannah's safety. Knowing when it was safe to speak up made a difference in her life. Speaking up when it is safe can affect your life too.

Technology Tips for Deaf Women

Technology gives us new and better ways of communicating and getting information. Things are changing all the time. Computers, pagers, TTYs, and other adaptive aids have changed how Deaf people get things done. Deaf people now connect around the world in a way that is visible and clear to everyone. Videophone technology makes it possible to use ASL for phone calls and see someone else sign back to you from across the country. There are many

continued

wonderful and accessible ways for Deaf and Deaf-Blind people to connect.

- Make sure you know how the devices work. Find out the safest way to use them. Abusers can use technology to learn about your conversations with your friends or other support people. An abuser is likely to try to control whatever you use to communicate with others. He may try to watch what you talk about or try to cut off your communication with others.
- Set up a code word or a signal with your friends or support people who call you on the TTY. That way you can be sure of who has called you. Or get Caller ID to help you make sure of the identity of the caller. But remember that when using the TTY relay system (dial 711) your phone number will be seen on the Caller ID machine, even if you have blocked your Caller ID from sending.
- When you call 911, make sure you use a TTY, telebraille, or telephone. For now, 911 cannot answer calls from DSL types of programs. Keep a phone line or make other safe arrangements to call 911 in an emergency.
- Many TTYs have a memory. Learn how to clear the memory of your TTY or telebraille. This way, your call will not be seen by the abuser.
- Think about where you keep printed tapes of TTY calls. Recent court decisions allow these tapes as evidence. Make sure that any risky TTY tapes are kept in a safe place.

Chapter 22:

△

Toward a New Life

In some chapters of this book, you have read quotations from women. They come from interviews with many kinds of women. All of the women were battered. And all of them got away from their violent partners.

It was not easy for these women to get away or to stay away or to make a new life. Some have had problems in their new lives. Most have gone through loneliness. Many have had hard times making ends meet. All of them have been discouraged at times. But none are sorry they left.

Many other women have been glad that they left abusive partners. Here, in their own words, are some of their reasons:

E.S.: "I'm no longer scared. Before, I could not even say what I wanted, express what I wanted. I was always in fear. Now, I like to go to school. I'm free. Even if I'm poor, I'm happy. I can feel happiness inside now."

Sandy: "Being mostly without a man for almost two years is really lonely sometimes and it's real depressing sometimes. . . . I'm in a space where I really appreciate me. I can believe that I can make decisions on my own. I can raise kids on my own. . . . I'm independent. I can deal with my kids without saying, 'Wait till your father comes home.'"

Patricia: "I'm living with a man who is totally the opposite of what I had before. It's give-and-take now. I've learned that. I live a normal life now. I have a normal relationship now. . . . I feel like I fit in the world. I'm not being kept in the basement."

Marilyn: "The best part of being away is being free, not having anybody criticizing me or telling me what to do. When I'm out and it's late, I don't have to call anybody to make up an excuse about where I am. At work I can concentrate because I'm not in crisis all the time. . . . I'm in the process of making major decisions, which I've never done. I never made decisions about what I'm going to do with my life. I'm wondering about that now, and I'm very slowly looking into possibilities. I'm asking for what I want. I never felt like I could do that."

That is their message to you. You, too, can change your life, and you can be free.

Resources

Suggested Reading

Inspiration: Guides on Survival and Stories of Women Who Survived Abuse

Cleghorn, Andrea. *Rosie's Place*. Acton, Mass: VanderWyk & Burnham, 1997. This is a short friendly book. As you read, you meet residents, staff, and volunteers in an unusual, inspiring shelter in Boston. Most of them are women of color.

Raphel, Jody. *Saving Bernice: Battered Women, Welfare, and Poverty*. Boston: Northeastern University Press, 2000. Bernice's life is a dramatic struggle. It shows the connection between battering, poverty, and public assistance.

Schwartz, Diane. *Whose Face Is in the Mirror? The Story of One Woman's Journey from the Nightmare of Domestic Abuse to True Healing*. Carlsbad, Calif: Hay House, 2000. Schwartz gradually claims her freedom from her husband. The reader learns lessons about gaining freedom along with Schwartz.

Men Who Batter, Children, and Custody

Bancroft, Lundy. *When Dad Hurts Mom: Helping Your Children Heal the Wounds of Witnessing Abuse*. New York: G. P. Putnam's Sons, 2002. Bancroft offers practical advice for mothers who have been abused. He shows how they can protect their children and help them heal.

Bancroft, Lundy. *Why Does He Do That? Inside the Minds of Angry and Controlling Men.* New York: G. P. Putnam's Sons, 2002. Bancroft explores the reasons that men batter, especially focusing on their characteristic of entitlement.

Bancroft, Lundy, and Jay G. Silverman. *The Batterer as Parent: Addressing the Impact of Domestic Violence on Family Dynamics.* Thousand Oaks, Calif: Sage Publications, 2002. Men who batter wives treat children in similar ways. The authors describe problems that come up in child-custody cases. They have advice for how to handle professionals who work in justice systems.

McHardy, Louis W., and Meredith Hofford. *Managing Your Divorce: A Guide for Battered Women: Child Protection and Custody.* National Council of Juvenile and Family Court Judges, 1998. This is an excellent guide to all legal aspects of custody.

Nicarthy, Ginny. *Getting Free: You Can End Abuse and Take Back Your Life.* Emeryville, Calif: Seal Press, 2004. With uncomplicated yet motivational language, this book contains all the tools and advice you need to help yourself recognize, respond to, and overcome domestic violence.

Teens

Levy, Barrie. *In Love and in Danger: A Teen's Guide to Breaking Free of an Abusive Relationship.* Seattle: Seal Press, 1998. This book is for teenagers who have questions about abusive dating relationships. It has many real-life quotes and scenarios.

Lesbians

Clunis, D. Merilee, and G. Dorsey Green. *Lesbian Couples: A Guide to Creating Healthy Relationships.* Emeryville, Calif: Seal Press, 2005. This is a practical book, written by two lesbian therapists, that covers a range of topics relevant to lesbian relationships.

Girshick, Lori B. *Woman-to-Woman Sexual Violence: Does She Call It Rape?* Boston: Northeastern University Press, 2002. Girshick combines personal stories of seventy women with studies. The women have experienced sexual violence from lesbian partners.

Rural and Native American Women

Websdale, Neil. *Rural Woman Battering and the Justice System.* Thousand Oaks, Calif: Sage, 1998. This book is written by a sociologist but is easy to read. It has many quotes from abused women, judges, and sheriffs.

Battered Women of Color and Immigrant Women

Agtuca, Jacqueline, in collaboration with the Asian Women's Shelter. *A Community Secret: For the Filipina in an Abusive Relationship.* Seattle: Seal Press, 1994. This book is a solid and powerful resource for Filipina women in abusive relationships. It addresses the subject of domestic violence in an empowering manner.

White, Evelyn C. *Chain, Chain, Change: For Black Women in Abusive Relationships.* Seattle: Seal Press, 1985. White offers supportive, straightforward information for African American women who are or who have been in physically or emotionally abusive relationships.

Zambrano, Myrna M. *¡No Mas!: Guía Para La Mujer Golpeada.* Seattle: Seal Press, 1994. Written in Spanish, this book provides advice and resources for women in domestic abuse situations.

Internet and Telephone Resources

Lundy Bancroft Website: Resources on Abuse and Recovery
www.lundybancroft.com
This website exists to support constructive action by women and men to end abuse in the lives of women and children.

National Coalition Against Domestic Violence (NCADV)
www.ncadv.org
National Office
P.O. Box 18749
Denver, CO 80218-0749
303/839-1852

National Domestic Violence Hotline
www.ndvh.org
800/799-SAFE (800/799-7233)
800/787-3224 TTY

Rural, Native American, and Immigrant Women

Family Violence Prevention Fund: The Facts on Immigrant Women and Domestic Violence
http://endabuse.org/resources/facts/immigrant.pdf
Fact sheets about immigrant women.

Hot Peach Pages
www.hotpeachpages.net
Domestic violence information in seventy languages. That's right: Seventy!

Mending the Sacred Hoop
www.msh-ta.org
You can find technical assistance here. It has articles and links to lots of important information on Native Americans, rural women, lesbians, immigrants, and others.

Rural Women's Advocacy Programs
www.letswrap.com
Information for rural battered women. Links and personal stories of survival.

The Rural Womyn Zone
www.ruralwomyn.net
This website is full of articles on many aspects of abuse. It includes information on Native Americans. It puts the topic of abuse in a larger political context.

ADWAS (Abused Deaf Women's Advocacy Services)

www.ADWAS.org

ADWAS has pamphlets, books, and films for Deaf women who are abused. They are easy to read and have lots of illustrations.

4738 11th NE

Seattle, WA 98105

800/787-3224 TTY (available spring 2006)

Disability Services ASAP (A Safety Awareness Program)

www.austin-safeplace.org/site/PageServer?pagename=progr am_disability_stopintro

Stop the Violence, Break the Silence Training Guide offers excellent basic information online.

Washington State Coalition Against Domestic Violence (WSCADV)

www.wscadv.org/projects/disability_protocols.pdf

Cathy Hoog's *Model Protocol for Safety Planning for Domestic Violence Victims with Disabilities* is a nineteen-page guide for advocates. But you, too, may find useful ideas. Then you will know what to expect in a shelter. You might ask for some of the things the guide suggests.

Acknowledgments

In writing the new chapters for this edition of *You Can Be Free*, we drew on many people. They included experienced advocates and women and children who have been abused. We have listed some of our informants only by first names, to preserve their safety. Errors, misjudgments, or omissions are our responsibility, but the following people made this new edition possible:

Abused women and children let us in on nuances of abuse that informed this updated edition. We have called them by these names: Anita, Anju, Asha, Beth, Carol, Cheryl, Janeese, Karen, Maryam, Michelle, Patsy, Rachel, Sachiko, and Tukata.

The work of the following people has furthered our own efforts, and some gave generously of their time to answer specific questions:

Connie Burk, Neha Chandola, Meg Crager, Scott Dungan, Elida Espinoza, Celia Forest, Kay Frank, Bob Free, Sandra Gresl, Louise Higgins, Leigh Hofheimer, Lois Loontjens, Vicky Miellie, Farhiya Mohamed, Linda Norris, Linda Olsen, Ward Orion, Andrea Parra, Lupita Patterson, Teryn Peroff, Anita Prasad, Laura Rebman, Mari Roll, Lyni Smith, Marilyn Smith, Carlin Tsai, Maria Verdin, Amber Vora, Ginny Ware, June Wiley.

Some agencies have generously shared specific resources. Others have indirectly informed and supported our work on these chapters. The following agencies have made the task significantly easier: ADWAS (Abused Deaf Women's Advocacy Services; Chaya; New Beginnings for Battered Women and Their Children; Las Amigas; Northwest Immigrant Rights Project; Refugee Women's Alliance (Re-Wa); Washington State Coalition Against Domestic Violence. We are also grateful for the work of Lundy Bancroft and Neil Websdale.

Cathy Hoog coauthored the chapters for women with disabilities and for Deaf women. They would not have existed were it not for her unfailing good humor, wisdom, and sensitivity. Her admirable traits made working on those chapters a special treat.

We appreciate Avalon's willingness to publish this updated edition, which focuses on issues faced by women whose situations have rarely been addressed by mainstream publications.

Avalon editors Jill Rothenberg and Marisa Solís demonstrated great patience and attention to detail, which made an enormous difference in the final product. They have been remarkably efficient in editing and managing the final stages of the book's production.

Index

About the Authors

Ginny NiCarthy has written and cowritten many books that have helped change the lives of thousands of women, including *You Don't Have to Take It!: A Woman's Guide to Confronting Emotional Abuse at Work; Getting Free: You Can End Abuse and Take Back Your Life; The Ones Who Got Away: Women Who Left Abusive Partners;* and *Talking It Out: A Guide to Groups for Abused Women.* Ginny began her work in the movement to end violence against women in 1972 as a founder and director of Rape Relief in Seattle. She later founded and directed the Abused Women's Network. For six years she wrote a newsletter on the international movement to end violence against women, and she is a member of the board of directors of Chaya, which serves South Asian women, and of the King County Coalition Against Domestic Violence, where she edits a quarterly e-newsletter. She sees her work with individual battered women as closely intertwined with other community, national, and international campaigns to stop abuse of power and to promote peace and justice.

Sue Davidson is a writer and an editor whose professional work since the 1970s has focused mainly on women's history and women's issues. Her books include the youth biographies *Getting the Real Story: Nellie Bly and Ida B. Wells; A Heart in Politics: Jeannette Rankin and Patsy T. Mink*; and *Changing the Game: The Stories of Tennis Champions Alice Marble and Althea Gibson*. She edited and contributed to *The Second Mile: Contemporary Approaches in Counseling Young Women*, and is the coeditor of *The Maimie Papers* and *A Needle, A Bobbin, A Strike: Women Needleworkers in America*. She was an editor for The Feminist Press at Old Westbury, New York, from 1974 to 1980, serving as a codirector of its multivolume *Women's Lives/Women's Work* series. A lifelong opponent of all forms of violence and injustice, Davidson's main affiliations have been with the War Resisters League, the American Friends Service Committee, and the American Civil Liberties Union. She is also a member of PEN.

Cathy Hoog is the Social Change Specialist at Abused Deaf Women's Advocacy Services, where she has worked since 1987, providing advocacy to Deaf, Deaf-Blind, and Hard of Hearing victims of sexual abuse and domestic violence in the greater Seattle area. She works in partnership with both the Washington State Coalition Against Domestic Violence and the Washington Coalition of Sexual Assault Programs in their projects to provide statewide accessible and appropriate services to victims with disabilities. She is the author of "Model Protocol for Safety Planning for Domestic Violence Victims with Disabilities." Cathy, who is Deaf and from a Deaf family, is a survivor of domestic violence.

Selected Titles

For more than twenty-five years, Seal Press has published ground-breaking books. By women. For women. Visit our website at www .sealpress.com.

Getting Free: You Can End Abuse and Take Back Your Life by Ginny NiCarthy, MSW. $16.95, 1-58005-122-7. This important self-help book covers issues such as defining physically and emotionally abusive relationships, getting emergency help, deciding to leave or stay, the economics of single life, and how to be your own counselor.

Inconsolable: How I Threw My Mental Health Out with the Diapers by Marrit Ingman. $14.95, 1-58005-140-5. Ingman recounts the painful and difficult moments after the birth of her child with a mix of humor and anguish that reflects the transformative process of becoming a parent.

In Love and In Danger: A Teen's Guide to Breaking Free of Abusive Relationships by Barrie Levy. $10.95, 1-58005-002-6. This clear and compassionate guide speaks directly to teens about what constitutes abusive relationships—emotional, physical, and sexual—and how to break free of them.

Real Girl Real World: A Guide to Finding Your True Self by Heather M. Gray and Samantha Phillips. $15.95, 1-58005-133-2. In this fun and essential guide, real girls share their experiences, discussing beauty and the media; body image and self-esteem; eating disorders and good nutrition; and sex and ways to stay safe and healthy.

Helping Her Get Free: A Guide for Families and Friends of Abused Women by Susan Brewster. $13.95, 1-58005-167-7. With a new introduction and updated resource section, this straightforward and compassionate book offers the information needed to help give strength to abused women.